D1760323

Withdrawn

CRY
AMANDLA!

CRY

AMANDLA!

South African Women

and the Question

of Power

June Goodwin

A fricana Publishing Company
a division of Holmes & Meier
New York   London

HQ
1800.5
.G66
1984

First published in the United States of America 1984 by
Africana Publishing Company
a division of Holmes & Meier Publishers, Inc.
30 Irving Place
New York, N.Y. 10003

Great Britain:
Holmes & Meier Publishers, Ltd.
131 Trafalgar Road
Greenwich, London SE10 9TX

Copyright © 1984 by June Goodwin
All rights reserved

Book design by Stephanie Barton

Photographs on pp. 42 and 94 by Norman Matheny, *The Christian Science Monitor*
Photograph on p. 160 by Enoch Duma
All other photographs copyright 1984 by June Goodwin

Library of Congress Cataloging in Publication Data

Goodwin, June.
  Cry Amandla! South African women and the
question of power.

  1. Women, Black—South Africa—Psychology.
2. Women—South Africa—Psychology.   3. Women in
politics—South Africa.   4. South Africa—Race relations.
5. Power (Social sciences)   I. Title.
HQ1800.5.G66 1984   305.4'0968   83-18374
ISBN 0-8419-0899-0
ISBN 0-8419-0911-3 (pbk.)

Manufactured in the United States of America

To my father and my mother

Contents

NO CHOICE

Acknowledgments

The political judgments in this book are mine, but to many people I owe special gratitude:

- Geoffrey Godsell, for the universality of his humanity,
- Beverly Gologorsky, who devoted her editing skills and her caring to the book to the nth degree,
- a woman who must be nameless, who buoyed me through difficult times and whom it is an honor to know,
- Joy Elliott, who lent a hand,
- JoAnn Levine, whose enthusiasm spurred me on,
- Cedric and Penelope Mayson, who gave me many good and useful ideas,
- Barbara Lyons, Tim Taylor, and Naomi Lipman for their astute and sympathetic shepherding of the manuscript,
- Benjamin Schiff, who encouraged me and made the last months of work translucent.

Above all, to the women who opened their homes and minds and hearts, I owe the entire book.

CRY
AMANDLA!

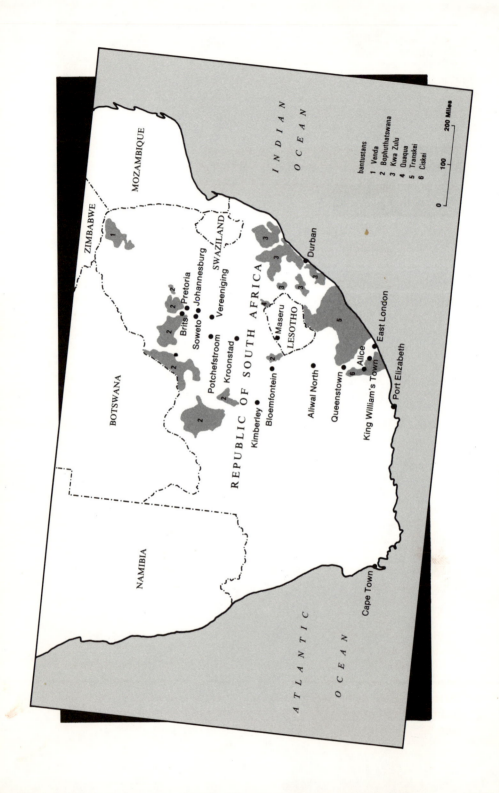

ZIMBABWE

MOZAMBIQUE

BOTSWANA

NAMIBIA

SWAZILAND

LESOTHO

REPUBLIC OF SOUTH AFRICA

INDIAN OCEAN

ATLANTIC OCEAN

1

2
2
2
2
2
2
2

3
3
3
3
3
3

5

6

Brits
Pretoria
Soweto • Johannesburg
Vereeniging
Potchefstroom
Kroonstad

Kimberley •
Bloemfontein •
Aliwal North •
Queenstown •
Maseru •

Durban

East London

Alice
King William's Town
Port Elizabeth

Cape Town

bantustans
1 Venda
2 Bophuthatswana
3 Kwa Zulu
4 Quaqua
5 Transkei
6 Ciskei

0   100   200 Miles

Introduction

"**A**mandla!"

The word for power, accompanied by a fist thrust high, is the new cry that crosses all African languages and marks a new generation of politics in South Africa.

It is a cry threatening to the white power structure of apartheid, a cry both exhilarating and frightening to blacks. It is a symbol of a turning point, of a new black militancy that has not died out since it surfaced in 1976.

In early June 1976, I visited South Africa for the first time. I went into the black township of Soweto—a white woman, without a permit, without knowing I was required to have one.

Only fifteen miles away, in the landscaped streets of Johannesburg, I was stunned by the hatred, the tension, the fear between black and white people. No white person spoke or sat with a black person. The hostility was palpable.

Two weeks later, the schoolchildren of Soweto made headlines around the world, fighting and dying for what had begun as a march for better education.

First as a teacher and then as a foreign correspondent I had lived in other parts of Africa. I had seen the most abysmal poverty. I had seen racism, colonialism. But apartheid was different from anything I had experienced.

I had assumed that apartheid in South Africa resembled racism in the American South, the negative response of white people to people of other colors. That assumption was not wrong, just extremely inadequate.

Before I left Nairobi for Johannesburg, I told my roommate, a black American, "Look, I'm going to be very objective about South Africa. Those white people must have reasons for what they do and I want to find out what they are." Only later did I learn how appalled she had been, although she said nothing at the time.

3

But I was a journalist. My formal education had taught me respect for objectivity. This meant fairness, honesty, and truth. It also meant no subjectivity. That was the definition, not the reality.

I lived in South Africa from June 1976 to January 1979. Before being permanently based in Johannesburg, I traveled around the country for eight months. I met black people in homelands, in townships; some of the people literate, some not. All equated apartheid with oppression.

I saw how black people were forced to exist and how much better the lives of white people were. I saw enough to need to find out more about the people who created and supported apartheid. Who are they? Why did they invent it? How do they explain themselves to others? What is the emotional content of a country that defends apartheid and considers itself to be in the twentieth century?

I did not go to South Africa to write a book. But the people I met and what I learned motivated me to do so. I wanted to share with others not only what is happening there, but how the people themselves perceive it.

Being a white foreign correspondent, I could cross the gulf between races and speak to black and white South Africans who do not speak to one another, not in depth, not any more, except for some—there are always a few.

I spoke to men and women, but I wrote about the women. They were representative of more than themselves and close to the heart of the society.

I met black women who could not imagine themselves demonstrating militantly in the streets, but who would not think twice about harboring and protecting a freedom fighter. Women who are masters at fooling the masters. Domestic servants in white homes who turn "stupid" to get what they need, while others turn "stupid" to keep what they have—but always to outsmart the baas, as the white masters were traditionally called.

And then I met Thenjiwe Mtintso, called Thenjie (pronounced Ten-jee) by her friends. She is the heroine of this book. Through her life she explains the tragedy that is today South Africa. By the time I met this dynamic woman, born in the township of Soweto, she was already a political organizer, a street fighter, in training full time to dismantle apartheid.

But she had not always been so committed and involved. She is two years younger than the 1948 implementation of apartheid. So, like her son, who was born in 1973, she has known nothing but a system of white rule that is deplored throughout the world and called a "crime against humanity" by the United Nations.

Thenjie was twenty-three before the true import of apartheid clicked in her mind. The instant it did, she was on the political barricades and became something of a legend among the South African security police.

The things she told me about her life were hard things to tell, and it was sometimes nearly impossible for me to ask. But she understood precisely why she needed to recall torture, death of friends, and all the emotions and reasonings of her development. She is totally committed to the abolition of a system that tried relentlessly to dehumanize and subjugate her.

I met her first in March 1977, three months after she was banned. She had learned much of her politics from Steve Biko, the father of the Black Consciousness Movement. In 1973 Steve had been banned, a heavily restrictive punishment limiting travel, work, and speech. Through Thenjie I was introduced by phone contact to Biko and I met him in King William's Town only a few weeks before he was killed. When I interviewed him, Thenjie could not be present because her banning orders restricted her hundreds of miles away in Soweto. Thenjie lived at King William's Town from 1974 to 1976. Biko, killed by security police in 1977, passed on to Thenjie and others living in King William's Town in the eastern Cape province the philosophy of black self-confidence that had grown in the late sixties and early seventies out of the University Christian Movement. Most of my interviews with Thenjie were in December 1978, January 1979, and in early 1980. She discussed both her personal and social outlook and her politics.

The Black Consciousness Movement was the 1970s phase of black opposition to apartheid. It was the descendant of earlier movements—the African National Congress (ANC), established in 1912, and the Pan African Congress (PAC), which had split off from the ANC in 1959. Both the ANC and PAC are alive, but are outlawed by the white government and operating underground. ANC subscribes to a nonracial policy, while PAC is black separatist. Because the Black Consciousness Movement believes blacks are the only ones who will help blacks, it was often considered a philosophical descendant of the PAC. However, since 1980 many former Black Consciousness advocates have aligned themselves with the ANC. The split persisted in late 1983—the PAC people coinciding with the National Forum Committee (NFC) and many in the United Democratic Front (UDF) being at root ANC supporters. The NFC and the UDF were operating above ground.

Several of the other black women I interviewed for the book knew Thenjie and respected her enormously, and a few of the liberal white women had heard of her from newspaper articles. But none of the women who supported the minority government had ever heard of her. In fact, they had not heard of Steve Biko until he was killed and an outcry went up from the world. To keep people apart is the aim of apartheid, and in this it has so far been very successful.

In all her life Thenjie held conversations with only three Afrikaners. Afrikaners are the Dutch-descended whites who were originally called Boers and who devised apartheid, declaring blacks to be citizens of rural, poor, tribal homelands even though many of them lived their entire lives in a white-designated area. Black cities such as Soweto are satellites to white cities; they are called townships and hold minimal legal status. Out of a total population of 29 million South Africans, 4.6 million are whites. Of these, 60 percent are Afrikaners; most of the rest are English-speaking whites of British descent.

It was imperative for me to show the Afrikaner women's points of view because they are the wives, sisters, and daughters of the men who invented apartheid and who now rule. It is a society content to be male dominated. But the Afrikaner women are not without responsibility for apartheid. They, like the men, gain materially from its continuation. Interviews with these women show what Thenjie is up against and reveal how the whites can cling to racist views and policies so roundly condemned by the rest of the world.

The Afrikaner women are friendly, gracious, and hospitable. I visited their homes in the suburbs. The home-and-hearth atmosphere is reminiscent of the 1950s American family in the Midwest when it was most nuclear—confined to its own, new back yard. Unlike black women, Afrikaner women share one language, one culture, and one history. Whatever their individual likes, dislikes, or particular personalities, it is their perception of apartheid that reveals most about them, their society, and, at times, their vision of the future. Obedience, not inquiry, is respected; too strong a dissent from the norms of the society is viewed as a betrayal of *die volk* (their people).

Most Afrikaner women do not like publicity. Those who speak here are among the more assertive. Even so, their public involvement is limited to influencing, not deciding, the issues. Although open and willing to talk, they would not completely share with me the content of disagreements among themselves. The conversation of the more intelligent seemed sometimes open and at other times shrouded. Had I spoken Afrikaans—the language that has developed from seventeenth-century Dutch—I might have delved more deeply.

Afrikaans is not a language spoken outside the country, and Afrikaners feel complimented when people learn it.

In this book I do not interview either colored women, as those of mixed black and white race are called under apartheid, or Asian women. Individual coloreds or Asians have had and will undoubtedly continue to have an impact on the political scene. But the two power centers remain the African and the Afrikaner.

The small group of English-speaking white liberals form a bloc that is virtually powerless politically, but which has a wide influence because of its use of the media and because of its wealth and international contacts. A few of these liberals would cheer Thenjie on in sympathy, but most of them would not be able to go all the way and break the laws that weave an insidious web around black lives. Although I found some of these women among the most intelligent and aware people in the country, Thenjie speaks to the liberal position with scorn. Most of those liberals who are upset by apartheid leave the country. Increasingly, however, the white English-speaking population that remains has moved to the political right as urban guerrilla warfare escalates: they now side for all practical purposes with the Afrikaners. Although the decades-old rivalry between the Boers and the English is still evidenced in bitter suspicions, the whites are drawing closer together. There are a few outstanding exceptions, men and women who, to varying degrees, follow their consciences in opposing the repression of individual and civil rights under apartheid. Many of them live in comfortable homes and have black servants. They are vocal publicly, active in organizations, and willing to discuss their work. They are for the most part not "leftists," as Afrikaners claim, but middle-of-the-road liberals.

A bit more liberal yet were several young white women I met, who maintain friendships with black people, who support the black struggle, but feel isolated. Because most forms of protest have been banned, they complain they can do little by themselves. And there is a tiny handful of whites, banned or exiled, who continue to work for black liberation. The whites who oppose apartheid to the extreme are a tiny minority.

One of the longest-running theater productions in Soweto during the 1970s was a play entitled How Long? How long until "freedom" from white domination? Ten years? Twenty? Can whites hold power into the next century? Will urban guerrilla warfare increase? Will black anger explode spontaneously throughout the country? Black people do not bother to predict; they only proclaim they will win: Victory is inevitable.

In less than a decade, white rule has been overthrown in Mozambique, Angola, and, most recently, Zimbabwe. Now, as one white woman said, "There is only South Africa. It is touching us."

White South Africans speculate about which course blacks will follow in the future. They don't often admit to one another that the war has already begun. However, the Afrikaner government, with help from Western industrialists, prepares for what it calls "total onslaught." Every bomb inside South Africa, every protest-related detention by the security police, every black attack on police or armed forces installations, is evidence of the increasing polarization between the races. The words of these women explain the reasons for that tragic splitting apart of South Africa. The political and emotional positions they held in 1978, 1979, and 1980 are still valid; in fact, they are even more written in blood than they were then. Their words will remain true for many more years, for the whites are not going to relinquish meaningful power without a prolonged fight.

Wherever white people gather in South Africa the fear of revolution is pervasive. Wherever black people gather, there is hope for *amandla*, coupled with a fear of violence. Along with death and destruction, which are ever-present in black townships such as Soweto, there lives a desire for life and laughter surpassing anything experienced in the placid, pretty white suburbs.

APARTHEID: THE SYSTEM AND AFRICAN REACTION

Steve Biko at the Zanempilo Community Health Clinic he set up outside King William's Town, August 1977

1

Origins of

Protest

**Black Consciousness has this outstanding effect of psycho-
logical freedom.   —*Thenjiwe Mtintso, 1979***

W e were driving very fast from King William's
Town to catch an airplane in East London. My
editor and I had just finished an interview with
the young black nationalist Steve Biko. The road was charcoal gray
with no center line. Hills and bushes rose and faded along the way.

People, dark as the night, walked along the road in the Ciskei
tribal "homeland." Now and then candles flickered from homes in
the distance.

Our headlight beams stabbed down the highway into the moonless darkness. A honey-colored dog dashed onto the road, swerved,
and stopped, eyes glittering into the headlights. He yelped, yelped,
yelped. We had hit him. Silence returned exaggerated. The driver, a
friend of Biko's, pulled the car to a halt on the left shoulder to be sure
the dog's body was not attached.

He climbed back in. We did not talk. The car resumed its speed
to catch our flight.

The war in South Africa is like that: people die, whites and
blacks, but mostly blacks. There is no choice but to go on.

Several weeks after our interview, on September 5, 1977, Steve
Biko was detained without charge and held incommunicado. Steve's
friends were not worried—he had been detained before and he had
come out before. On September 11, 1977, Steve Biko died of head
injuries inflicted by the police, who were to claim that he beat his
own head against the wall of his cell. Only with his death did the
outcry arise both in South Africa and abroad, for Biko was admired

by a few influential people overseas. When the brutal manner of his death was revealed at an inquest, much of the world was appalled.

On his coffin two carved fists ripped apart a chain between the wrists.

Although we talked to Steve Biko for only a short time, we could see he was not embittered, despite the death of friends at the hands of security police; he was extraordinarily articulate and incisive in assessing the character and dynamics of the South African society. His fearlessness and equanimity left an indelible imprint on our minds. He had been "banned" in 1973, and this peculiar South African restriction prevented him from traveling out of a small area, proscribed his being quoted in the South African press, and prohibited his talking to more than one person at a time. Nevertheless, he spoke with the two of us, along with three other people, in a room at the medical clinic he had set up with colleagues. He told us that he still believed there was time for dialogue and peaceful actions to force change in South Africa. He said, however, the guerrilla tactics of some blacks would be useful, too, in eradicating apartheid.

Biko was a large man for a black South African. He had an open smile with a small gap between his frontmost teeth. Although he was now thirty he had by the age of twenty-seven formed political organizations; he had testified eloquently at the treason trial of two Black Consciousness friends and written extensively on the meaning of the political philosophy he had helped formulate:

> Black Consciousness is in essence the realization by the black man of the need to rally together with his brothers around the cause of their oppression—the blackness of their skin—and to operate as a group in order to rid themselves of the shackles that bind them to perpetual servitude. The interrelationship between the consciousness of the self and the emancipatory program is of paramount importance. . . . Blacks are out to completely transform the system and to make of it what they wish.

What did Biko wish? In another passage from a compilation of his writings (*Steve Biko, I Write What I Like* [New York: Harper and Row, 1978], p. 49 and p. 98), Biko said, "In time we shall be in a position to bestow upon South Africa the greatest gift possible—a more human face."

We tried to determine if Steve Biko and his friends were in any way directing the political protest that was still rumbling across South Africa more than a year after June 16, 1976. The first students were killed on that day in the black township of Soweto, outside Johannesburg, hundreds of miles from King William's Town; after that the marchings and deaths had raged throughout the country.

Whether the estimated seven hundred to one thousand deaths over a two-year period were in Cape Town or Bloemfontein, the unrest was called "Soweto." Biko denied any direct command connection with "Soweto," saying it was a spontaneous explosion by the students. He indicated, however, that the effect of the Black Consciousness Movement was crucial in the genesis of the protestors' militancy. He said that a greater clash over apartheid was inevitable. "All we can do is minimize the conflict," he said.

Steve Biko grew up in extreme poverty with plans to become a doctor. Attending the medical college for blacks in Durban in the early 1970s, he was forced out because of his political activity—but not before he had led the black South African Student Organization (SASO) to break its alliance with the white liberal student group, the National Union of South African Students (NUSAS). He had latched onto the tenet of apartheid that blacks must stay separate from whites and had adapted it for Africans' political use. The starting point of Black Consciousness—"Black man, you are on your own"— denied blacks their traditional reliance on liberal whites for help in opposing apartheid. Biko reasoned that liberals will always urge gradualism and never encourage the full revolution blacks need.

At first the Afrikaner rulers were delighted with the split because it snubbed the white liberals, descendants of the British who had humiliated the Afrikaners' ancestors by winning the Anglo-Boer war at the turn of the century. Gradually, however, government officials realized that Black Consciousness was snowballing and threatening apartheid law and order. A month after Steve Biko was killed, the government banned all Black Consciousness organizations. But Biko's influence on the struggle for black liberation did not end with his death. He had passed on to others the understanding, courage, and sagacity needed to carry on the work.

One of those who would do so was Thenjie Mtintso. During my first two meetings with Thenjie, encounters several months apart, I did not know that she was a top Black Consciousness leader and a close friend of Biko's. Although political activists were open and warm once they determined you would not expose them to the police, they were initially cautious in testing individuals. During my first meeting with her, arranged by a friend, I was researching a story about being banned in South Africa. Thenjie's banning orders* were then only three months old.

That cool March evening in 1977 I left my apartment among the high-rise buildings of Hillbrow and strolled a mile or so away toward

*Appendix A.

the appointed meeting in my friend's house. Walking past urine-tainted dark alleys that vein this most cosmopolitan area of Johannesburg, I watched the last of the day-shift maids and cleaning women drift toward the bus and train stations for their journeys back to Soweto. Black watchmen, clutching long wooden knobkerries, edged into their nighttime nooks. Shop lights snapped off. In the sky, the four kite-stick stars of the Southern Cross lit up over the tallest skyscraper of downtown Johannesburg.

In his apartment, my friend had taken the usual precautions for banned encounters: the constantly tapped phone was smothered under a pillow; curtains were drawn against the police, who occasionally staked out his apartment; the bedroom door was left ajar to facilitate a quick departure, if necessary.

There were three people in the dimly lit room. My friend, his wife, and Thenjie, a small, thin, black woman wearing a maroon pantsuit, the platform shoes then in style, and large, dangling, clip-on earrings. She drank apricot juice and lounged on the upholstered beanbag chair, watching me from behind dark tinted glasses.

Without preliminaries we began talking. I could quote her, she said, but not by name. Then she told me how the banning orders against her affected her life. Later I was to learn how frequently she ignored the orders, just as Biko had, and continued her political activities with panache.

During a second interview in July the same year, she agreed to meet me with Geoffrey Godsell, the late foreign editor for the *Christian Science Monitor*. Thenjie wore the same maroon pantsuit but no earrings. When I commented, she reached into her pocket and cupped them in her palm. She had read my article in which the anonymous banned person was identified by her earrings. She had removed them.

That night she attempted to teach Geoffrey to say *amandla!* He tried and failed; she laughed in a voice unusually deep for such a small woman. Her three-year-old son Lumumba's hands were tiny, but she told us he already said *amandla!* and raised his fist high above his droopy, dreamy eyes. It had been only a few years since blacks had first folded their handshakes into the lifted tight fist—the *amandla* gesture—detested by the white authorities.

As we said good-bye, Thenjie abruptly exclaimed, "You should give me your earrings." I unfastened the wires and handed them to her. We walked to the car. At the door, Geoffrey raised his arm in a broad fist. *"Amandla!"* he said. Thenjie grinned and said, *"Awethu!"* ("is ours"). A few months later she was imprisoned and I did not see her again for almost a year.

In September 1978, when Thenjie had been out of the Fort prison one month, we met briefly in the garden of another banned person. She greeted me with that sweet hug black women give each other, brushing arms and hands lightly across each other's breasts as they pull apart. She pointed out she was wearing my earrings. A friend in prison had pierced her ears. At five o'clock the next morning, the security police rapped on Thenjie's door in Soweto and took her away without any charges for the fifth time. Her family learned several days later that the security police had transported her first to John Vorster Square police station headquarters and then to a large prison in Potchefstroom, a farming and university town about 150 miles south of Johannesburg.

When she was released in late 1978, my interviews with her began in depth. She started by telling me what the Black Consciousness philosophy and Steve Biko meant to her political development. I encouraged her to talk about the Black Consciousness community at King William's Town, where she lived from 1974 through 1976. I wanted to know the social attitudes of these revolutionaries, not only to pinpoint the conservatism in the society but also to draw a more human portrait of this woman whose courage was awesome. I asked her about the black men's attitude toward women and about her thoughts on sexual relations between blacks and whites in order to probe to a more emotional level. This was an issue more explosive when discussed by South African whites and I wanted to contrast Thenjie's attitude with those of the white women.

"Steve was a great talker. I was the greatest listener," Thenjie said. "He was not a great reader. He thought people should read, but he didn't have time. You wouldn't find Steve sitting at home in the evening reading a book. But he had been involved in politics a long time and had done a lot of reading before he came to King William's Town.

"Steve never sat down to say, 'Look Thenjie, I'm teaching you politics.' But I knew his thinking. Whatever I am today, or at least 70 percent of it, I owe to Steve.

"When Steve was killed, I did what I thought he would do. Someone came to tell me he was dead. I didn't break down. I got into my car, drove to town, phoned King William's Town, and asked what they needed from me. Then I phoned the guys around Soweto and told them we had to meet that night. I knew that Steve would have said at that moment that we would be silly not to exploit his death. 'I am dead; you cannot do anything about it. You should start using my death.'

"It was only after I was detained in October 1977 that his death hit me very hard. In that cell in the evenings, I would think about Steve. When I looked at what his death meant politically, it just wrecked me, because I saw him as a messiah, our liberator. He was not a superman; he had his ups and downs like anyone, but I could not think of any man who could lead the blacks like Steve; I could not think of any person who had his analytical and political mind. I could not see anyone who would be followed and obeyed like him.

"I did not want people to see me breaking down and I deceived them into believing I was very strong. In fact, I was trying to console them. If I broke, lots of others would too; so I had to be strong. But when I did break down about his death, I also realized I was not doing myself or the struggle any good because my outlook was emotional. I would say to myself: Let us look for arms and fight; there's no time for talking; if they kill a Biko, what will they do to the rest of us?

"Steve's death still makes me feel lonely, but I can't allow depression. I learned from Steve to be a survivalist (sic)."

Thenjie said that after his death she didn't know exactly what political move he would have suggested besides using his death to highlight black opposition to apartheid. "But I know he would still have felt that there is room for peaceful change in this country, if we strategize correctly. We can still hit the Afrikaner where it hurts— not violently. He was that type of person.

"Black Consciousness has this outstanding effect of psychological freedom," Thenjie explained. "We have been taught that we are nothing, an aberration from the normal, which is white. I don't know whether it's automatic, but in a black man there is just that sickness of feeling. He may not say, 'I feel inferior,' but he is always wondering. Steve said, 'You have been trying to emulate whites. You have lost your values. You have been uprooted. Now go back to your roots and from there you can emerge as a man in your own right.'

"There is a difference between our struggle and the American black struggle," Thenjie said. "In America, blacks must fight as a minority. Here we are the majority. The country is ours."

Thenjie's mother, Hannah Mtintso, was born in 1897 in Pondoland, part of the Transkei tribal reserve about five hundred miles south of Soweto. Mrs. Mtintso's father was an Anglican minister, having adopted the Christianity of the missionaries in Transkei. "Hannah, a slave name," Thenjie said kiddingly. But Thenjie's first name is Ethel, and older friends still call her by her own slave name. Thenjie's father, who died when she was three, was Guna Makabeni, but until Thenjie was in her late twenties her mother led her to believe that her father had been Mr. Mtintso, actually the father of

her older half-sister, Liziwe, and her half-brother, Phillip. After Mr.
Mtintso died in the late 1940s, Mrs. Mtintso met Guna Makabeni, but
the two never married. Mr. Makabeni had a reputation as an eloquent political speaker and organizer for the secretary of the garment
workers' union and as a member of the oldest black nationalist
movement, the ANC.

Like her mother, Thenjie is Xhosa. She was born in Soweto but
declared by apartheid to be a "citizen" of Transkei, the first tribal
homeland to be declared an independent country by South Africa
and recognized only by South Africa. Born in 1950, she grew up like
many children in Soweto, poor, in a one-room shack. There was no
one to look after her while her mother worked, except an old woman
who got drunk and ate Thenjie's food.

"I don't think I'd be able to pinpoint exactly when I started being
politically conscious," Thenjie said. "I can just recall my childhood
was not unlike the childhood of the ordinary black child in Soweto.
But I have a feeling that we were the poorest type of family. We
stayed in a place called 'Shelters,' which would be the equivalent of
Crossroads, the squatter camp near Cape Town today. Shelters was
eventually demolished and we were moved to Orlando East, where
we still live. I must have been about five, and my mother was working as a nurse's aide patching uniforms in Baragwanath hospital. My
brother and sister were at school."

When Thenjie was six or seven, her mother sent her to a tiny
town in Transkei called Mpozolo to live with her aunt. "We were so
poverty-stricken that I thought my mother must have thrown me
away. Transkei was worse than anything I had ever experienced. I
was used to urban poverty; now I was finding rural poverty."

In Transkei, Thenjie attended Clarkebury Methodist Church
boarding school, where she showed promise as a speaker and joined
the debating team. She remembers taking the negative side once,
when the debate topic was "Western Civilization Is a Boon to Mankind." Student politics at that young age revolved around complaints about food and living conditions. "I was not very popular
with the administration, although they liked me as a person," she
recalled. "They thought I was the one who was influencing the students." Undoubtedly she was, since she told me she has never been
shy. But Thenjie's political awareness was still minimal.

Her political education developed more from observing her sur-
roundings than from reading. "I always had the feeling I must grow
to be something to help alleviate suffering," she said. "But the suffering was still limited to my family. I used to think about being a
doctor so my mother could stay at home and not go and patch those

uniforms for the nurses. The Clarkebury school cost 52 rands [about $62] a year. Lizzie, who was paying for the school, was sickly and I think my mother was earning 35 rands [$40] a month. And then, I was not well. I had arthritis. The joke of it was that our matron at school interpreted it as hysteria. She was not educated."

"Was she white?" I asked.

"No, black. I cannot imagine how she thought painful joints were equal to hysteria. There were nine of us at the school with the same thing. We were supposed to be wanting men. Medical care was nil."

Thenjie left Clarkebury in 1966 because of ill health and because her sister could no longer afford the tuition. "My political awareness began with the fact that I had to leave school because I did not have enough money. I don't regret it. I feel this has built me, this suffering. Perhaps if I had not suffered at that stage I would not have been interested in bringing about change."

The Mtintso house in Orlando East on Letsatsi (sun) Street is a standard four-room Soweto house of two bedrooms, a living room, and a kitchen, with a wooden outhouse in the left corner of the back yard, back to back with the neighbor's outhouse. Residents can see almost everything in Soweto because, except in the better-off areas, fences are usually wire. To get to the house one must weave a car over the rutted dirt road to the middle of the block and swing through the tall pipe-and-wire gate to park at the right side of the house. In summer, bright floppy flowers pop out in the grassless front yard like nosegays dropped at random. Occasionally someone hoses the dirt to lay the dust.

"In our street, Letsatsi Street, there was a man who was arrested in the early sixties for his political activities. He has not yet come back from prison," she said. "My sister, Lizzie, and this man used to have some nocturnal meetings; they'd talk and I'd listen. He gave me the book *No Easy Walk to Freedom* by Nelson Mandela." The book is now banned and ANC leader Mandela is in prison for life for his activities against apartheid. "But the book had no impact on me since I was only about fourteen then," Thenjie said.

When Thenjie returned to Soweto, she had only a Junior Certificate, a document showing she had passed the equivalent of tenth grade. By now her sister was ill in a hospital and her mother was trying to maintain the family. Nevertheless, Thenjie attended school for a short time in Soweto. "A Mrs. Minsky paid school fees for me to go to Morris Isaacson high school, but I left as early as May 1968, because my mother was about to be pensioned off and it was urgent that I get a job."

"Who was Mrs. Minsky?"

Thenjie did not know. She said she had searched for several years to find the woman to thank her. She guessed her benefactor belonged to Black Sash, a white, liberal, English-speaking women's organization opposed to apartheid. "I didn't know about Black Sash then. She was just a good white.

"When I was about seventeen, I was told I was intelligent and could become a doctor. But circumstances such as poverty and being black in this country made that impossible."

At the age of eighteen Thenjie was forced to find a job. Her first employer was a Chinese man named Ho Tong, owner of a factory in Johannesburg that printed words and designs on ashtrays, glasses, and ballpoint pens.

"We were supposed to call him *Baas* Ho Tong. And we did," Thenjie said.

In her spare time Thenjie took correspondence courses from Damelin "college" to obtain her matriculation or high school diploma. Her sister died in 1969.

"I've never been attached to anybody more than to my sister. She took care of me; she was a mother, a sister, a friend, everything to me. After she died, I felt an obligation to her to become a doctor, to be something."

After great financial struggle and with a partial grant from the mining conglomerate Anglo-American, she entered Fort Hare University in 1972, at age twenty-two and older than most of the other students. Thenjie's political activity began with SASO and the 1972 Fort Hare student strike, which demanded a representative council for the students. These councils would multiply in universities and high schools across the country and become the major organizing centers for black political action between 1976 and 1978. In 1973, after Thenjie had been forced out of the university because of her political activities during a second student strike, she felt anger toward whites.

"It was not really hatred. I think it was irresponsibility and not understanding issues. Even at that stage I had no complex against whites and didn't hate them."

A group of SASO students roamed Johannesburg, Thenjie among them. "A very silly clique now that I look back at it." They would straddle the width of a sidewalk jammed with pedestrians heading toward the bus and train stations at rush hours.

"We used to walk in the street and not move apart as whites approached. They got real scared, which amused us, and we would tell them we were *swart gevaar*—Afrikaans for 'black peril.' I interpret it as perhaps a childish stage, but it can be traced to anger."

By Thenjie's own reckoning the 1973 student strike had completely politicized her. "The strike lasted a month and involved violence. Students who tried to do assignments were beaten. I found I was a good speaker. That's how I became 'popular' with the security police. I realized that, to be effective, students had to organize off the campus."

After SASO leaders decided parents should be involved, Thenjie and others toured the country to explain their position. During this tour she met Biko, who was already working with black community programs in King William's Town.

That year he was banned to Ginsburg, the black township near King William's Town. The outside world, including foreigners, beat a path to his door to discuss Black Consciousness and to see the small community that lived by its philosophy. King, as the community was called, became a black nationalist center. Although in the early 1970s press coverage of the Black Consciousness Movement was sketchy, the government had been following it since the late 1960s. Many government attempts to stop its ideas from spreading had not succeeded.

Thenjie went to live in King in January 1974, after she was finally forced out of Fort Hare.

"I didn't know anyone but Steve, so I stayed in his house in Ginsburg. Anyone who didn't have accommodations arrived and remained. It's quite amusing: Steve had this double bed and sometimes there'd be ten or fifteen of us, so we'd sleep across the bed, men and women. There was no question of he's a man, I'm a woman. We were just brother and sister. We slept in one room. You slept in whatever position you found yourself, sitting or horizontal.

"There was a King life style. We were not different in ideology from our colleagues in the Transvaal (province). But we were distinct in approach; we were not moderate."

I asked if tribal differences emerged among the blacks living in the Black Consciousness community at King.

"In a sense the tribes are not that culturally different," she said. "We've got the same customs and our languages are mutually understood. You will find there are minor differences between Pedes and Zulus. But they are not differences we can classify as relevant. The Pedes circumcise their women and the Xhosas do not."

I asked if Biko's outlook on women or that of the other Black Consciousness men was traditional.

"To Steve, a woman was a woman. This did not mean she should not be involved in politics or was unintelligent or should not show initiative. If you failed an assignment, you just failed, not because you were a woman. They elected a person to a position, not a woman or man. There was no discrimination.

"But if we were not discussing serious politics, the men would say, 'We are hungry, make food.' They never cooked for themselves.

"In terms of girlfriends, a man was supposed to have them. And an African man is, what do they say, polygamous by nature. In the African culture it is allowed. Steve felt we couldn't waste time discussing whether a man should have ten girlfriends or two, as long as it did not affect his political activity or himself in any way.

"I remember Siyolo Solombela, a second doctor at the King clinic. He had so many girlfriends, we called the clinic an institution. If one popped in, Siyolo would say, 'You have not been invited. There should be order in an institution. Order means you must be told when to come.'"

"Did women live with many boyfriends?" I asked.

"No, it would not do for women to be as loose as men; I could not think of having a boyfriend. Steve never said, 'Don't have one,' but I knew I couldn't risk it. I could not misbehave in any way as a woman. Loose morals were unthinkable.

"Once while living in King I left to meet Ralph Mgijima [the father of her son, Lumumba]. We drove to his parents' home in the *bundu* (bush). I felt awkward. I was not supposed to meet the parents until we were married. At the time, in 1973, Lumumba was six months old and living with my mother in Soweto."

Following custom, Thenjie did not look into the eyes of any family member, but kept her eyes down. She did not eat when offered food, which was also customary.

When relatives asked who she was, Ralph teased. "Who does she look like?" he said, meaning Lumumba, but they could not guess. He told them. Immediately, the uncle was summoned, as was proper, to record an important family event. Thenjie retreated to the kitchen, as was the custom, and remained there until they departed.

Soon after, Ralph, an active nationalist, was forced to leave the country and go into exile. They had not married.

"Could you marry and still work politically?" I asked.

"If I were to get married it would have to be with a man who shared my political thinking. I could not imagine myself having a husband who went out to a meeting while I sat home to cook for him. Because I want to be where things are happening, we would have to go together. I'd still do the things that are done by an African woman. I'd respect my husband, which is why he'd have to be very intelligent. If he were not, I would despise him.

"I would not follow my husband to find out if he had a girlfriend. I'm jealous and possessive but I've got confidence in myself. I wouldn't mind his having affairs. I'm sure that I can have a man and feel I possess him wholly, as a person, knowing that he has a girlfriend or a wife.

"If I find a man has another relationship I would ask if he was in love with that person; if that was the one he wanted, I would withdraw completely."

I asked if she considered the black woman doubly oppressed —by the system and by the black man.

"It never occurs to me I am being oppressed by any black man. The westernized black woman does, of course, feel oppressed by the male having many affairs. But the African man says, 'I've always been polygamous; it is my custom.' The ordinary black woman does not feel repressed by tradition."

To Thenjie, black women in South Africa today must say that freedom is their priority.

"The problem is that black women are not yet politicized enough to realize we are in a state of war. Unfortunately, the men have developed, but the women have been left behind.

"I'm not so westernized that I can say I'm equal to a man. I still feel that men are superior to women. I know I contradict myself because I dismiss certain men as stupid. But even if I can do something better than him, I must respect him as a man. I don't know if you see?"

To Thenjie, sex between blacks and whites is anathema.

"I cannot imagine being caressed by a white man. I would shudder. In South Africa, when a white man touched me, my response was not antisexual but antiwhite. I never looked at a white man in a sexual context. I guess I feel this way because I was born into a situation where color plays such an important part."

Thenjie was in her twenties before she knew any white people. The white attitude toward black/white sexual relations is expressed in the enforcement of the Immorality and Mixed Marriages Acts. However, black women seem unaware of or, like Thenjie, are unconcerned with the depth of white terror on the issue. From the black female point of view, it is a peripheral problem.

Thenjie dismissed as minimal the number of white women who fall in love with black men. Instead, she assessed the power relationship between black women and white men.

"The black woman ends up the loser because the white man buys her. I grew up with this girl and we suffered together. She failed matric, not because she was stupid but because she was poor. She said to me, 'Thenjie, how long have we been poor? I'm tired of being poor. Go, my dear, and raise your fist. I'm not against your raising your fist. But from today, I'm not going to be poor and live in the slums anymore.' That was in 1975. She said, 'White men have money to throw away,' and she was going to take that money. She said it was unfortunate she had to use her body, but the black man was not going to give her anything. She divorced her husband and now lives in a white area." Thenjie recalled that while speaking, her friend smoked a cigarette in a golden holder.

"My friend said, 'You know, that man wakes up in the morning and gives me 20 rands for the day; that 20 rands would work for two weeks in Soweto. At month's end, he gives me 300 rands [$345] to shop.' Now, that's material gain," Thenjie concluded. "And, of course, I can't say he doesn't love her, but I have to be suspicious."

Father Aelred Stubbs is an Anglican minister from Britain who lived in Johannesburg in the 1970s and knew both Steve Biko and Thenjie well enough to explain an important difference between the two. "Thenjie had never been part of the liberal white student scene. That cooperation had gone out before she got to Fort Hare," he said. "It's sad that many of these kids never had a chance to mix with whites the way Steve had. Steve always fraternized with the liberals at the same time he was knocking them so hard. He simply wouldn't give up a friendship. He could do that, but Thenjie had to find her way into dealing with whites. Steve and the Black Consciousness community established themselves and Thenjie as people in their own right who must be respected and listened to."

There are few places for blacks to sit in downtown "white" Johannesburg

2

Johannesburg,

Apartheid's White

Lie

F rom the air, the earth around Johannesburg stretches flat and baldish and red-orange. The geography of the gold-mining reef on which the city is built resembles Kansas City and Australia. It is unlikely terrain for guerrilla bush warfare. Yet the reef is full of targets: power lines, dynamite factories, gold mines, nuclear development plants, oil pipelines, police stations, two bulbous radio-television towers, shopping centers, the mammoth Voortrekker Monument in memory of Boer pioneers, military bases—and people—over a million whites and probably twice as many blacks.

Johannesburg, the magnet in the heart of South Africa, throws the compass needle of apartheid into a frenzied quiver. Nearly one quarter of its nighttime population is black: servants in white homes; migrant workers in gigantic hostels. And by day, when residents from townships commute into the factories, the black population is even larger. Johannesburg has sucked blacks out of rural areas like millions of iron shavings. They cluster around the mines and industries, living mainly in Soweto, the black satellite city fifteen miles southwest.

Thousands of Soweto residents are migrant workers. But thousands of others were born in urban areas. They have never seen a tribal homeland. Nevertheless, these urban blacks do not legally belong permanently in or around areas designated white.

If the police stop an unemployed black in a white area, he is charged, detained, then sent either to prison or to a rural homeland. The police are vigilant. They conduct raids in all white areas of the country. During 1982, police arrested someone under the pass laws every two and a half minutes. According to the Institute of Race Relations survey for 1982, the total number of arrests made for pass-law offenses, by police and administration board officials, was 160,600. This was up from 117,518 in 1980.

Since 1961 at least eight million blacks have been arrested or prosecuted under the pass laws. Since 1956 1.3 million have been deported to tribal homelands; between 1960 and 1974 an estimated 1.4 million blacks were forcibly moved off white-owned farms where they once used the land in return for their labor; between 1948 and 1979, 439,329 Africans were removed from so-called "black spots," land traditionally owned by Africans but arbitrarily transferred to whites.

Most whites do not call this repression. "It is influx control," they explain, "the law in South Africa."

In Johannesburg as in other large cities, black and white people are near each other every day. But few whites see black people as they do other human beings.

"Lay-dee, I tell you, I know our natives." Lay-dee is an expression of an Afrikaner speaking English to an English speaker. Sometimes the tone is almost polite but more often bureaucratic, exasperated, or legally nit-picking.

"Lay-dee, they just don't think like we do. I grew up with them. I spoke their language when I was a boy. I know. They couldn't run a country, at least not this one."

This is racism, yes. But it is the racism of apartheid. And apartheid is not this society's drift into traditional bigotries. Apartheid is the most codified and elaborate blueprint ever devised for human relationships. It covers every facet of life.

Afrikaners developed the system to meet their own economic, political, and social needs. They used "separateness" to eliminate the threat of black competition in the labor market. They believed and taught their children to accept the division of people into groups as the will of God.

Afrikaners claim the group ideology has its roots in the Bible. They swear they live and will die for their theological and racial beliefs. They share their beliefs freely with whites visiting South Africa. They do not, however, wish to count out loud how many ways they benefit from apartheid.

One of the prime short-term benefits of apartheid for whites is to push to the sides of their minds the awareness of the sheer numbers of blacks versus whites. In 1983 the Human Sciences Research Council, a government body, projected that blacks are expected to outnumber whites in urban areas of South Africa by four to one by the year 2050—only two generations away, the pro-government newspaper, *The Citizen*, noted. Today it is generally reported that blacks number slightly fewer than whites in the cities.

There are now a total of around 29 million people in South Africa: 4.6 million are white. Of the whites, 60 percent are Afrikaners, 40 percent are English-speaking. There are roughly 21 million Africans, 750,000 Asians, and 2.5 million racially mixed people referred to as "coloreds."

The colored people stand at the interface between black and white, in an apartheid limbo. They live in separate areas from Africans and their home language is usually the Afrikaans of the ruling whites. Some Africans view coloreds as wanting to "be white," but many of the young ones call themselves black and have aligned themselves firmly with the Black Consciousness Movement.

"You are writing this book," said the man, his eyes narrowed, his lips tight. "Make it say the white man came to our country. Nine months after he arrived, there was a colored baby. That's all. That explains it."

But to the Afrikaner, apartheid is literally a miracle. It happened on earth two and a half centuries after the first Dutch settlers landed on the Cape in 1652. There, they found the Khoisan people, derogatorily called the "Hottentots," and the African Bushmen—tough, barefoot nomads who carried water in ostrich-egg shells. The whites brought Christianity and guns. They hunted the Africans as if they were kin to the tailless rabbits that dart about like furry rocks on top of Table Mountain over the beautiful harbor of Cape Town.

At the turn of the century, when whites fought one another in the Anglo-Boer War, the British flattened the Boers. Over a quarter-million Boers—most of them women and children—died in British-supervised internment camps.

In 1918, three Boer or Afrikaner men concerned with the poverty and low self-esteem of their people formed Jong Suid Afrika (Young South Africa). Two years later it became the Broederbond (Brother Bond), described then as a semireligious organization. In 1921, it instituted secret membership and rules.

Today, although the military is gaining in ascendancy, the all-male, all-Afrikaner Broederbond is the sub-rosa governing power of

South Africa, dominating as well the English-speaking whites. Nearly all top government men are members of this body, which is accountable to no electorate.

To Americans, the Broederbond recalls the Ku Klux Klan, with one overwhelming difference: the Broederbond's twelve thousand members run a country. In South Africa, they are the "establishment," holding power on all levels of society: government, media, church, schools, police, railways, post office, etc.

In the mid-1930s, a core of the Broeders formulated the apartheid plan. However, it did not pass into law until after World War II. During that war many Afrikaners, including the late former Prime Minister John Vorster, refused to fight against Hitler and were detained by the then South African government. Others who would become the enforcers of apartheid went to Germany to study Nazi indoctrination methods.

In the 1948 general election, the Afrikaner National Party, guided by the Broederbond, came to power. With D. F. Malan as prime minster, the Broederbond emerged with the apartheid plan in hand.

The system is divided into petty and grand apartheid.

Petty apartheid is more than the customs of prejudice. It is law. Under petty apartheid:

It is illegal for a black to stay overnight in a white's house without special permission.

It is illegal for whites to serve blacks liquor.

It is illegal for blacks to go into most theaters, restaurants, movies, white sporting clubs, country clubs, churches, public lectures. Special permission can be sought for churches, lectures, and sports clubs.

It is illegal for a person of one race to address people of another at a political meeting where a majority of the audience belongs to another race.

It is illegal for a black to ride in a white bus or train.

It is illegal for blacks and whites to perform on stage together.

It is illegal for blacks and whites to have sexual relations.

It is illegal for blacks to use white public toilets, although in the white areas where they work and shop the number of black facilities is inadequate.

It is illegal for blacks to go to white private schools, except with special dispensation. They cannot go to white public schools.

It is illegal for blacks to enter the white side of any store.

When foreigners comment adversely on the rules, Afrikaners point to changes made by the Nationalist government in the past few years. No more "whites only" signs in elevators; no more black and white sections in post offices; some theaters may have multiracial audiences; a few more hotels and restaurants have opened to blacks. Because of international pressure, there are more multiracial sporting events—but permits are always needed. In urban areas blacks may now own their houses under ninety-nine-year leases, but never the land beneath them.

During the 1977 election campaign, Foreign Minister Pik Botha said he was not prepared to die for a sign in an elevator. Blacks, too, say they are not prepared to die for a sign in an elevator. They say petty apartheid is only filigree on the grand design.

And it is minor compared to grand apartheid, the master plan for maintaining white minority rule in South Africa.

A government-printed map of grand apartheid, titled "Bantoegebiede en Bantoedorpe in Die Republiek van Suid-Afrika en Suidwes-Afrika soos in 1975" (Bantu Homelands and Bantu Towns in the Republic of South Africa and Southwest Africa in 1975) outlines where blacks and whites live. Only it doesn't. Cape Province shows no blacks at all. But the smallest child sees blacks in Cape Town plucking grapes in the vineyards or plowing mielies (corn) in the Orange Free State. How can blacks be and not be in Cape Province?

In fact the map is lying. It does not list the hundreds of black townships, like Soweto, which fringe the white areas, where nearly half the black population lives.

Each black township is larger than the white area it services. The white areas are permanent, with full, legal status. The black townships are temporary. Under grand apartheid, all black people, including those born in townships, are assigned to tribal homelands at age sixteen, when they must register to obtain their pass books.

The map shows only the homelands—or bantustans, as they are also called. They form a scraggly string of islands around the white center of the country. These homelands for twenty-one million blacks comprise only 13 percent of the land surface of South Africa. The remaining 87 percent of the land is controlled by the 4.6 million whites.

The reality of living in a homeland is death. It may not be the quick extermination of masses by gas chamber; but it is internment, with death from starvation and disease. Contained within the homelands are overcrowded shacks on land that is impossible to farm, thousands of people with stomachs distended from malnutrition, and constant reminders of inadequate health care and education. The token budgets allotted homeland administrations from white

Pretoria do little to relieve the poverty. When black people speak of genocide, they are referring to the law that ships so many so far to die. In 1983 the head of the University of Natal pediatrics department predicted that thirty thousand children could die in a year because drought had made the living conditions even worse than usual.

When a black man is recruited from a homeland to work in a white area, his wife and children cannot accompany him. When a black woman from a homeland finds a job in the white area, her husband and children cannot go with her. The homelands contain the elderly, the children, and the wives without husbands, as well as those "resettled" there.

In the late 1970s and early 1980s, the South African government declared four homelands "independent countries": Bophuthatswana, Venda, Ciskei, and Transkei. Transkei is geographically the most cohesive land mass and the only one of the ten black homelands to claim some of the country's thirteen-hundred-mile coastline. Vacationing whites drive through the eroded, crowded, poor tribal reserve to see the Indian Ocean's long blue waves crash up onto the rocky shore around Port St. Johns. Plans were reported in late 1983 for a fifth homeland to be declared independent in 1984, Kwa Ndebele, whose main economic asset is the export of labor to "white" areas in South Africa. This would mean another 1.3 million people will join the more than eight million blacks who have been stripped of their South African citizenship. Blacks assigned to these "independent," economically unviable entities have no citizenship rights in South Africa. They are foreigners. They can be and are shipped out of white areas permanently.

Under the government's "Bantu education" plan, many schools for blacks were shifted to the homelands. Because many urban schools are overcrowded, black parents must often send their children to rural boarding schools or to none at all.

In 1976, when schoolchildren exploded in anger and then died over the issue of their education, the government was paying 48.55 rands ($55.83) per year per black child's education and 654 rands ($747.50) per year per white child's education. That means white children were subsidized thirteen times more than blacks. Moreover, blacks had to pay school attendance fees and buy school books whereas whites did not.

In October 1981 a government commission to examine the status of education reported that the spending differential had not changed much—113 rands (about the same in dollars) for each black child and 1,075 rands for each white. The 1976 ratio was 1 to 13; the 1981 ratio was 1 to 9.5.

Only three out of every one thousand blacks ever finish high school; and 63 percent of black workers have never attended any school.

One of the main complaints of students who haphazardly continue to protest, especially at the universities, is that not only do blacks have access only to inferior and segregated education, but the schools, from elementary through university, are unnecessarily divided along tribal lines.

In fact, one of the pillars of apartheid is division, and despite a 1981 recommendation by the government commission to unify the black, white, Asian, and colored systems, the government, as it had since the mid-1950s, refused. In 1955, the Nationalist government rejected the recommendations on black education made by its own Holloway Commission, and built two black universities with tribally separate education plans: the University College of the North at the isolated farm of Turfloop, twenty-five miles from Pietersburg, and the University College of Zululand in Natal.

Fort Hare University in Cape Province, where Thenjie attended classes for a short time, was built during missionary days, originally serving Africans from as far away as Kenya. Zimbabwean Prime Minister Robert Mugabe attended Fort Hare, which enjoyed a high scholastic reputation. The student body included coloreds, Indians, and Africans. However, in the late 1950s, under "Bantu education," staff members were dismissed, colored and Asian students phased out, and the Broederbond took control. Fort Hare is now predominantly for Xhosa students.

Black students refer to the three universities as "bush colleges" because of the remote location and the inferior education. As if to stress no change of education policy, the government in 1982 established two more such universities in the tiny impoverished homelands of Venda and Quaqua.

In 1978, the term "Bantu education" was changed to "Education and Training Department." But the basic intent of the education remains the same: to train blacks to serve whites.

Since it became law, no aspect of grand apartheid, with the homelands policy as its centerpiece, has been abandoned or substantially modified. And after the 1976–1978 black uprising, Broederbond documents revealed the intent is to expedite the plan, while altering some of apartheid's petty practices.

In the city, grand apartheid is not obvious. The poorest are out of sight, far away in homelands. Johannesburg is not like Addis Ababa or Calcutta, where poverty and disease are nearly overwhelming. The visitor to Johannesburg sees women wearing the latest fashions. Western brand-name cars, electronics, foods, and cosmetics are available. Large modern shopping centers abound.

At Cafe Wein in a shopping mall in Rosebank, a white suburb of Johannesburg, black nannies carry white babies on their backs; black waiters serve white customers. The scene could resemble a wealthy Dallas suburb. Except in Rosebank the waiter and nanny can never sit where whites do. They could be arrested. If their pass books do not have an urban and a job classification, they can be shipped to a rural homeland, the way an illegal alien is deported. But the waiter and the nanny, like the white person, were born there.

The average white in South Africa is seldom aware of the laws of apartheid, for they apply to blacks for the convenience of whites. The lie of apartheid is that Johannesburg is a white city, that Cape Town, Durban, Pretoria, Bloemfontein, etc., are white. This lie, which essentially says blacks do not exist, is comic in the sense of the emperor's having no clothes, but tragic, in that so many people have been tortured, killed, and exiled for pointing a finger at the naked injustice.

On the tombstone of Steve Biko is the slogan "One Azania, One Nation." The phrase, besides adopting the name that the Pan African Congress (PAC) gave South Africa, explains and refutes the essence of the apartheid plan: one large, powerful white nation and ten splintered, powerless black nations.

For years blacks have fought for recognition of their rights and their existence. After the ANC, the granddaddy of all the nationalist movements, was formed in 1912, protest was generally moderate. Then in 1944 the ANC Youth League was formed; in 1952 the Defiance Campaign of civil disobedience was launched; in 1959 the PAC split off from the ANC; in March 1960 the PAC organized the Sharpeville pass protest, which ended with sixty-seven people killed, most of them shot in the back by police; then ANC and PAC formed military branches to their political organizations; in June 1964 ANC leaders Nelson Mandela, Walter Sisulu, and Govan Mbeke were sentenced to life imprisonment on treason charges; both ANC and PAC were declared banned organizations.

Not until the very late 1960s did the Black Consciousness Movement rise up from the post-Sharpeville black quiescence. It took two years of police repression of the protests and the banning of Black Consciousness organizations and leaders to dampen the flame. But, unlike conditions after Sharpeville, black organizing has continued, especially in trade unions, the churches, the National Forum Committee, and the United Democratic Front.

Significantly, there has been a resurgence in the underground ANC. On March 20, 1983, a car bomb exploded in Pretoria near military headquarters killing 17 people and injuring 188, many of them civilians. Until then the ANC had targeted only property. Oliver Tambo, the exiled president of the ANC, said afterward, using biblical terms that so many of the many Christians in South Africa would understand: "We have offered the other cheek so many times there is no cheek left to turn."

The desire for freedom by the black majority is tenacious. It withstands banning, detention, and deportation to homelands. Black political organizations have been forced underground. But in the streets of South Africa's cities a premonition of change fixes on the soul.

John Vorster Square, security police headquarters in Johannesburg

3

Security for

Whites

L ike halves of a two-chambered heart, one black, one white, the cities of Johannesburg and Soweto throb together. Situated at the center is John Vorster Square, the police headquarters building and grounds. From here the whites enforce their laws.

Highways splay outward from the ten-story building in all directions. The M1 sweeps north to rich suburbs where fewer than one million white people live; it continues north to the capital, Pretoria, a tidy bureaucratic town where most of the white men wear military and police uniforms. South and west, the M1 cloverleafs into the Great Reef Road, which threads through an industrial area to Soweto, where nearly two million black people live.

In 1978, John Vorster Square was the subject of an Amnesty International report on torture in South African prisons.

Blacks who have been tortured are reluctant to talk about it. "Read *The Trial* [Franz Kafka]," one man told me. "It describes our situation exactly."

Those who did relate their experience spoke in an even tone, watching the listener's eyes, sometimes smiling incongruously—a reflex to lessen the listener's pain, one man explained.

In John Vorster Square the ninth and tenth floors are reserved for interrogation. There, police hold black prisoners out of the top windows by their feet; place guns in their mouths and fire blank bullets; pull out their large toe nails; knock off edges of teeth with pliers; yank out pubic hairs; apply electric shock to genitals.

"Any complaints?" the police ask on their routine prison pa-

trols. The law requires them to ask. "Any complaints?" "No complaints," a fifty-year-old Soweto man replies, standing naked in his
cell.

In November 1977, an illuminated object was seen suspended at
roof level outside the Market Theater, one mile from John Vorster
Square. A sculptured mummy, spread-eagled and fluorescent against
the night sky, it was part of an art exhibition paying homage to real
men and women who had "fallen" out of prison windows.

At John Vorster Square, where I went to interview a top inter-
rogator, Warrant Officer Roussouw escorted me through the base-
ment and up the back entrance. She directed me to a sparsely
furnished waiting room with windows and door of frosted glass. She
wore not a uniform, but a dress, black nylons, and plain pumps. She
frisked me and spread the contents of my purse across the table.

Captain Arthur Benoni Cronwright entered, glancing back to
order tea. He had shiny black hair and wore a kelly green suit of
synthetic material. I was forbidden to take any notes during the
hour-long interview.

We sat down, the tea in front of us. Captain Cronwright demanded to know how I had heard of him and why I would approach
a man in such a position.

I told him several blacks had informed a white friend about his
campaign to convert prisoners to his born-again Christianity.

"Who really told you?"

"I just gave you my answer."

He didn't pursue it. Besides being advised of him by my white
friend, I had heard from several black men that they had been tortured under his supervision; one man died under his interrogation.

Captain Cronwright talked about being an evangelical Christian,
how important his religion was to his life.

"When people are born again, they talk in tongues. You would
think they were drunkards. They are. They are drunk with the glory
of God. The best communication is with God, not with people."

I asked him how a Christian can justify killing.

"The Bible says you can kill," he said, and repeated it. "The
Bible says you must drive Satan out by force; you must destroy
Satan." He pulled a small pipe from his pocket and Warrant Officer
Roussouw found a match for him. She sat with us throughout the
interview. Cronwright and I sat in cushioned chairs; she sat above us
in a straight-backed chair, very still, as though waiting to be photographed.

I asked about Steve Biko's death. He did not believe what he read in the paper. "I don't believe what people say. I only believe what I hear from God."

After the interview, Officer Roussouw watched me repack my belongings from the table.

"Are you a born-again Christian?"

"You didn't come here to ask me questions," she replied.

"What is Captain Cronwright's first name?"

She refused to tell me. I would have to phone him back, she said.

She ordered the ninth-floor steel doors opened and escorted me outside to a parking lot beneath the overpass of the M1 Highway.

No information on prisons may be given to the public. The laws are strict. It is illegal to write about prisons unless the police have cleared the material. In addition, local newspapers cannot quote banned people or report freely on strikes or other unrest. Since the 1977 banning of the black paper, *The World*, freedom of the South African press has steadily eroded.

Censorship of the printed word occurs throughout the world; but the censorship of *people* is peculiar to South Africa. Since 1953, more than fourteen hundred people have been banned for five-year periods, including forty Black Consciousness leaders in 1978. "It amounts to paying for your own imprisonment," said a banned person.

A white woman, Helen Joseph, who was eighty years old in 1983, was placed under house arrest in 1962. She was the first person so treated. In 1983 she was unbanned but remained "listed," which meant she could not be quoted in the press. She adamantly refuses to leave the country while her old friends, Nelson Mandela, the national leader of the ANC, and Walter Sisulu, also an ANC leader, remain in prison.

In South Africa the security police or censorship board ban anything: books, movies, magazines, T-shirts, the thumbs-up gesture of ANC, or one war game.

A game entitled "South Africa: The Death of Colonialism" was seized and banned in 1978. I had purchased the game at a university bookstore in the United States and given it to a person who showed it to a journalist. The game was described in a page-one story in *The Sunday Express*, with emphasis on the fact that in the mock fight, only black nationalists can win. Publicity around the incident brought to light a fast-growing white society of regular war-gamers who met at Windsor Park Club in Johannesburg to play these games.

Since 1948, the Afrikaners have enacted more than sixty security laws to enforce petty and grand apartheid. These include the Internal Security Act, the Terrorism Act, the Banning Act, and the General Law Amendment Act.

John Dugard, a professor of law in Witwatersrand University in Johannesburg, has outlined three categories of detention-without-trial laws: (1) those that permit detention and interrogation in isolation, (2) the 180-day detention law, which allows detention of witnesses, and (3) the preventive detention law.

Laws in the first category, particularly Section 6 of the Terrorism Act, violate a number of basic canons of criminal justice:

- They exclude habeas corpus and the power of the courts to investigate the lawfulness of a person's detention.
- They exclude the right of an arrested person to be informed of the cause of his or her arrest.
- They deny the right of an arrested person to be visited by a lawyer.
- They deny rights accorded to prisoners awaiting trial: provision of reading and writing material.
- They permit inhuman and degrading treatment.

In 1978, under apartheid, there were

- 261 people detained under security laws
- 50 people banned
- 149 people shot and killed by on-duty police
- over 100 prisoners awaiting trial who died in police custody
- 403 people wounded by police gunfire
- 76 political trials
- people hanged, one every fourth day

The figures come from the Institute of Race Relations. The year 1978 was not unusual. In 1981, 620 people are known to have been detained in South Africa, including the tribal homelands of Transkei, Ciskei, and Venda. Of these, 95 were released, 226 were charged, 180 were still in detention, and 297 were unaccounted for, as of January 1982.

Those figures are only for detentions under security laws. Thousands of blacks are jailed every year for not having their pass books in order. On any day approximately 100,000 blacks occupy South Africa's jails either awaiting trial or already convicted. Many prisoners are hired out to farmers, construction companies, and

businessmen, who pay from 27 cents to $2.18 tariff per black per day
to the prison. The prisoner receives no money.

A liberal white woman commented: "Something that black people have taught me is the capacity human beings have to endure and
survive inside of terrible situations."

The Afrikaner legal system and those who administer it are usually scrupulous about following the letter of the law. The laws themselves, however, they do not question. Hence the more laws enacted,
the more trials that are carried out under wide license that sometimes seems a total lack of law.

During the 1977 Pretoria inquest into Steve Biko's death, a
song—half hymn, half Gregorian chant—was heard in the room,
soothing the hot summer air. The audience quietly began the singing
while sitting in the former Jewish synagogue, the site of the inquest.
When the spectators left the room for recess, they formed a large
group and sang, walking past the Afrikaner cops. The songs became
more militant, taunting. Police tapped their feet to the tunes, ignorant of the insulting meanings.

At a political trial in the Johannesburg suburb of Randburg,
young black students were led out the back of the building into a
waiting police van for the return ride to the fort prison. Parents
crowded around, crying. For most, it was the first look at their children in a year. They knew the students had been tortured. From
nearby, voices rose in freedom songs. From inside the van, the students responded: their arms pushed through the round gun sights,
their fists clenched in frozen *amandla* salutes.

Most freedom songs refer to slain or imprisoned warriors, such
as Black Consciousness leader Biko or ANC and PAC leaders.

I asked Thenjie if black nationalists sang the American civil
rights song, "We Shall Overcome," and she said, "Ya, but we laugh at
that song because it is sung here by the white liberals. They are
saying they will overcome, justice shall prevail. It is a good song, but
it's not ours. It's not quite a liberation song; but we sing it in our
gatherings because other people like it.

"Africans are people of the drums from long ago, so in our music
we find happiness, solace," Thenjie said. "When black workers sing
in the streets, they usually sing, '*Amabhulu ngodem*,' which means
the whites are evil. A white will stand there smiling at the tune."

New lyrics are born all the time, with the tunes often taken from
church hymns. One Khosa song, a favorite of Thenjie's, is
"*Mabawuyeke Umhlaba Wethu*":

> They must leave our land alone
> We the children of the soil are fighting for our land

We the children of the soil are prepared to die
for our land

Let them, the oppressors, leave our land alone

Let Africa come back
Let Africa come back.

AFRIKANERS

At the Voortrekker Monument near Pretoria, Boer pioneer Andries Pretorius looms over a grounds keeper

4

Chosen by Themselves

A choir of 250 Afrikaner schoolchildren, accompanied by the National Symphony Orchestra, performed in the Johannesburg City Hall. The choral work—"The Assault"—celebrated 1979, "The Year of Preparedness." It described the effect of an anarchist's physical and moral attack on white South Africans:

> *The Children's Choir:*
>
> This fair-haired child,
> how will he stand against the storm
> in this dark south, so European, so white,
> his legacy and ancient light refined and
> trimmed by order law, and form?

> *The Anarchist:*
>
> I, neo-Marxist, am anarchist, am terrorist.
> Your fate is sealed:
> you are my hostages,
> my target for shot and hand grenade.

> *The English Preacher to Anarchist:*
>
> How cunning your tactics.
> Your thoughts corrode and panic the mind
> while your bombs explode,
> destroying, polluting God's earth and air.
> Suspicions and doubt make our deeds despair.
> Your primitive rhythms that drop and lurch and
> batter the creed of our holy church are futile, fruitless.
> You'll not succeed.

> *The Voice of a Man:*
>
> Enough of this sort of hypothesis.
> Our ramparts are steady preparedness.
> Let Young South Africa speak.

When it was over, Julie Frederikse, an American journalist for National Public Radio, commented: "The contradiction between the change in attitudes urged by Afrikaner politicians and the values imbued in Afrikaner youth has yet to be confronted."

Thenjie, who has comforted herself so often in prison with freedom songs, would not be able to hear this choir of fair-haired children, but she knows the effect of the white ideology on her life.

Shortly after Thenjie was taken by the police to Potchefstroom, I began research for this book. Although she was locked behind bars, her spirit and her perspective went with me as I interviewed Afrikaners who would consider her a terrorist. Many of them might not have talked with me had they known that I knew and admired her. Even the most liberal of the five Afrikaner women whose voices are heard in the following chapters said of Steve Biko that there must have been a reason he was detained without being charged.

When I asked these women what they thought of Biko, if they would like to be black in South Africa, and did they support apartheid, Thenjie was in my mind. When one woman mentioned Potchefstroom because she had lived there, I thought of a certain prison.

I couldn't tell these women that loud clicks on my phone meant it was tapped by the police, that I had talked with at least twenty-five people who were banned, that the authorities detested some of the newspaper stories I had written.

Fear, already pervasive among these women, would have made the interviews more difficult, if not impossible, had I laid all my cards on the table. As it was, I pushed the most right-wing of the women as far as I could without jeopardizing communication.

There is a genuine, though often nebulous, terror among Afrikaners that their enemies are all communists. The fear is not without some cause, even though it is inflated beyond all reason. The ANC maintains an alliance with the banned, pro-Moscow South African Communist Party, and the recent takeover by black socialist governments of Angola, Mozambique, and Zimbabwe has convinced average white South Africans that they are being surrounded by godless communism. Some businessmen are less alarmed, for I met in Luanda, Angola, a white South African employee of an international corporation who was selling copying machines to the new socialist government because, he said, "Where there is any bureaucracy, documents need to be copied." That man had flown from Johannesburg to Lisbon to Luanda to sell his machines, mingling in the Tropicana Hotel with East Germans setting up Angola's secret police system. But to the average white South African the notion of a communist takeover is a persistent dread, kept alive by radio, television, and newspaper propaganda.

During the "Soweto" uprising of 1976 and 1977, many young students had begun to reason that if white South Africans feared communism so much, perhaps, for that very reason, it must be a good thing. However, they were as ignorant about communism as were whites because all books on the subject are banned.

The Afrikaners' antidote to communism is their version of Christianity, born centuries ago in their flight from Catholic persecution in Europe and now used to justify apartheid as the will of God. South Africa is the most Christianity-oriented country on the African continent. But Christianity in Soweto and Christianity in the Afrikaners' Dutch Reformed Church of two million followers do not seem to emanate from the same Bible.

The communism/Christianity clash among Afrikaners explains the society's reaction toward two of its most prominent opponents of apartheid—Bram Fischer and Beyers Naudé, two names often on the lips of the women I interviewed.

Bram Fischer, leader of the South African Communist Party and a lawyer who defended ANC leader Nelson Mandela in court, died in Pretoria in May 1975, after being imprisoned for life. To Afrikaners he is a traitor of the first order. Steve Biko said Fischer was the only white whom blacks view as a hero.

Beyers Naudé, a former Dutch Reformed minister who was once a member of the Broederbond, was banned in 1977 for his activities with the Christian Institute. The institute, with a membership of fewer than two hundred, assisted blacks in their community programs and was the only white organization banned in 1977 along with the Black Consciousness organizations. Naudé knew Steve Biko but not Thenjie, and the Christian Institute aided the medical clinic Steve set up in King William's Town.

Today Naudé lives in a suburb of Johannesburg, attends a Dutch Reformed Church regularly as a lay member, and is often visited one-by-one, to comply with his banning order, by foreigners and a few Afrikaners who consider him an exemplary Christian. In 1983 many banning orders were lifted by the government, but Naudé's were left in force and due to expire in 1985.

Most of the Afrikaner women I interviewed do not question the justice of Beyers Naudé's banning. They murmur, "There must be a reason." They accuse: "He left his people."

Fear of social ostracism is the special hell for the Afrikaner people. But Naudé, a man with a gentle sense of humor, is not tormented by his own ostracism. He advises Afrikaners that they will have no real peace until they choose as he has, and he speaks to them in the theological language they understand.

One of the best ways to approach a conservative Afrikaner woman is to appeal to her to talk about Christianity. I had used it to gain access to the security policeman Captain Cronwright at John Vorster Square. I also was allowed to interview the most right-wing of the five women in this book on condition the topic was Christianity.

At no point in either interview was there a complaint that we had veered off the topic although both discussions were heavily political. The Afrikaners' Christianity and their politics are so intertwined they are virtually indistinguishable.

Afrikaner women claim as their legacy the independent spirit of the pioneer Boer farm woman. But almost all of them think as their men think. In a National Party pamphlet, "Women, Our Silent Soldiers" (see Appendix B for complete text), the clarion call reads:

> Because we as women are believers, we work for our Party. We are conscious of our calling and therefore do our best. . . . We are not afraid. . . . We move forward with our menfolk, we demonstrate our loyalty to our Party, we are aware of the circumstances in which we find ourselves—the total onslaught against us as a nation.

In the same pamphlet, the prime minister is quoted:

> If ever there was a woman in the world's history who was called upon to serve, inspire and support her husband and her child, her nation and her country, then her name is: Woman of South Africa.

The white men who rule the society would not tolerate white women questioning their role. It is difficult enough that blacks are dissatisfied.

An Indian man observed, "It's amazing—about Afrikaner women. I've seen them around their husbands; they become so subservient."

"Afrikaner women do what they like; our husbands can't stop us. We have a few laws, but they don't hamper us," an Afrikaner woman said in defense of her society.

The wife of an Afrikaner police detective said, "Women can do a lot; they can change the world, really. But South African women are very apathetic. They are comfortable and very scared."

One way I tapped quickly into another fear of Afrikaner women was to ask them if they thought the Immorality and Mixed Marriages Act was necessary. Under the law, passed in 1948, more than ten thousand people have been convicted for having sexual relations "across the color line." From July 1979 to June 1980, 276 people were charged under the law. The Dutch Reformed church publication, *Human Relations and the South African Scene in the Light of the Scripture,* states in relation to racially mixed marriage, "Factors . . . which would eventually destroy the God-given diversity and identity would render such a marriage highly undesirable."

In Potchefstroom—there is Thenjie's prison town again—there exists, paradoxically, a group of Afrikaners called the Doppers, who have spoken against the Immorality and Mixed Marriages law. These theologically conservative adherents of the Gereformeerde Kerk, the smallest of the three Dutch Reformed churches, claim that the law violates biblical teaching since the Bible nowhere forbids racially mixed marriages.

In 1977 and 1978 the tiny Dopper group, Koinonia, took this stance and was forced by the authorities to cease activity. An English-speaking Calvinist working with Koinonia commented on how quickly the Afrikaner members caved in. "They are still more afraid that *Ooma* (grandma) will not speak to them on Friday."

"Afrikaner women were the ones who wanted the Immorality Act," a white male South African journalist said. "They didn't want their men with black women. Mixed sex happens all the time in the *platteland,* or rural areas. Sex is behind all of it, you know—behind apartheid. Sex is the only area where the Afrikaner men consider blacks superior to them. They think that all Africans want is to get into their wives and daughters."

Every year or so, rumors spread, picked up by the international press, that Afrikaner leaders are planning to scrap the law to promote change in attitudes. But quickly the rumors fade and the leaders hastily retreat.

The five Afrikaner women in this book range from the political right, with Gabrielle Malan, who supports apartheid totally, to Christelle Marais, who, with her husband, joined the liberal opposition party in Parliament.

Mrs. Malan is a religious lady with a steel backbone who devotes her time to reinforcing the Afrikaners' conviction of their God-directed right to rule South Africa. She is physically lovely and coldly gracious. Many Afrikaners do not speak English and wouldn't dream of talking to a foreign journalist. In this respect Mrs. Malan is not really on the extreme right in her society.

Freda Van Rooyen is the opposite of Mrs. Malan in her ebullience, more in the tradition of the earthy Afrikaner pioneer woman. She is more tolerant of people who disagree with her point of view and fervently tries to explain the Afrikaner to others. She does not say that she supports apartheid and yet, when pressed, she admits she believes in "influx control" and other elements of the system. She is a public relations expert for the Afrikaner. If not entirely convincing, she is at least warmhearted, volatile in conversation, and efficient in small crises.

Susann Wessels is a sophisticated, wealthy woman with refined European taste in furniture and art. There is none of the Boer pioneer trekker left in her.

Christelle Marais is not considered to have betrayed "her people," as Beyers Naudé did, despite belonging to the opposition liberal party. She has an interest in art and theater and a naïveté about the broader politics in South Africa.

Most fascinating of all, perhaps, is an Afrikaner woman who asked to be nameless for this book. She is maternalistic toward blacks and has performed many good deeds on their behalf, mostly by helping them to lessen the bureaucratic strictures of apartheid. One would like to think this woman is the heart of what could develop into love in the Afrikaner. But she is very, very rare. She made tears come to my eyes several times.

I doubt, however, that tears would come to Thenjie's had she listened to the woman, for the fear that Afrikaners voice is nothing compared to that faced so often by Thenjie. Thenjie would probably dismiss the woman's cringing before the opinion of her own society as cowardly and even immoral because of the woman's awareness of apartheid's injustice.

I sometimes felt almost schizophrenic in South Africa, shuttling from the black society to the white, listening to the people who should be talking to one another, coming to understand why blacks will turn more and more to the gun, and growing aware that some of the whites I talked with might eventually be the targets.

The world of these Afrikaner women is one starkly separate from Thenjie's. Thenjie could not enter it. I could because I am white. Such a thin layer is the skin, such an abyss have the Afrikaners created between black skin and white.

Come. While we question the rulers, imagine that Thenjie is sitting invisibly by, listening to her "enemy," assessing whether there is an alternative to war.

Gabrielle Malan in her Northcliffe home

5

In the Name

of Her

God

The best would be to do what they do in Japan—move
people with bullet trains into the (white) working areas by
day and take them back to their homes at night (in the
tribal homelands). I don't see why this country can't do it;
we've got the money. But, of course, this is a large country,
so it would be more difficult. But this would be the ideal
thing.   —*Mrs. Gabrielle Malan, 1978*

I was in the office of a Western news agency in downtown Johannesburg. Light mustard-color slag heaps
from the gold mines were visible through the south
windows. I was surrounded by whirring teleprinter machines and
stuttering rows of tiny lights on a large bank of computers.

On the television screen a church choir of white children sang a
hymn from the Afrikaners' Dutch Reformed Church.

A correspondent for an American paper, glancing at the screen,
remarked, "I don't understand how they can believe the things they
do."

I understood. I was from the fundamentalist "Bible Belt" in
Oklahoma, where religious exclusivity was taught. It begins with the
children. They learn that Ham, Noah's son, was cursed for seeing his
father naked and drunk. Ham was banished to the wilderness. "A
servant of servants shall he be unto his brethren." Ham's skin grew
dark and he became the ancestor of all Africans. Therefore, dark is
less spiritual than light. When blacks become more spiritual, their
skins will lighten.

And so a similar story is told in the Dutch Reformed Church, Gabrielle Malan's church. Her husband is a *dominee* (minister) of the largest of the three Dutch Reformed churches in South Africa. He is a member of the Broederbond. At first Mrs. Malan refused to see me but finally agreed, saying we would talk only about Christianity.

I drove to Northcliff, a rich suburb of Johannesburg. The figs were heavy and ripe on the trees. Servants from the whites' houses were picking the fruit and offered to sell me some. Flowers draped fences along the road. The Malans' yellow brick house stood like a solitary honeycomb on a stark, green lawn. Instead of the usual forbidding fence, grass and space separated the Malans' home from those of their neighbors.

Nearby, Dominee Malan's gray-brown church shafted skyward like a thick sword welded to the earth. The architecture was typical Afrikaner—concrete and monumental.

Dominee Malan earns from 700 to 800 rands per month ($805 to $920). His house is provided free by the church congregation.

Outdoors, some servants from surrounding homes loitered in the sun to gossip.

No black has ever told Mrs. Malan how much he hates apartheid. Nor has she seen a black fist raised in an *amandla* salute, except in photographs. She would never know blacks like Steve Biko or Thenjie.

In Northcliff she does not confront the black struggle for liberation. Not yet.

In the Malans' entrance hall hangs the family crest, DEUS ARX MEA (God is my fortress) emblazoned on it. In South Africa Dominee Jan Malan's family extends back seven generations, originating with French Huguenots run out of France by Catholic persecution. Malan is now a common Afrikaner name. Mrs. Malan's mother was Irish and her father an Afrikaner, a "mixed marriage" rare at the time, but "in these days it is a bit more common."

Mrs. Malan guided me into the living room. Slim, with blue eyes and blond hair, she sat on a tall-backed, dark chair, a white crocheted doily behind her head. On the antique table was a photograph of one of her three grown sons. On her desk she keeps the Bible, which she reads every day. She said she prays constantly and prayed for me the morning of our interview.

"Do you believe it is the men who run this society?" I asked.

"Yes, I think so." She spoke almost wistfully. "They make the decisions, even in the church. We haven't got the kind of democracy you have in American churches, with women taking big positions. I find the South African women, I don't know if it's laziness or lack of insight, but they're not keen on taking positions."

"Are they passive?"

"No, they're satisfied. It could have to do with the religion, the Old Testament type of patriarchal system with the father the head. Because they are so religious, they remain satisfied with the patriarchy."

"Do you find it frustrating?" I asked.

"Sometimes . . . a little bit; you've got to have permission for every move you make in the church. That is a bit difficult. You'll find it in any fundamentalist society. The Bible Belt people. You'll find they don't divorce; they might like to, but because the Bible is against it, they won't do it.

"In a way, of course, I think it's a good thing. I was listening to a tape on 'The Church Through the Ages' the other day. It was a shock to realize a lot of these sects were started by women who went completely off the road because of emotionality. I said, 'Oh, God, I must remember never to be emotional.' We are inclined to be more emotional. It was a little warning again to me not to move too fast. You know, I think with my heart; I do think emotionally."

"What's wrong with that?"

"There's nothing wrong with it, it's just not level-headed. I ask my husband's advice. He can give me an overview. Eventually I would make up my own mind, but he would give me a bit of vision which just perhaps would alter my decision. I accept that. Of course, he's very wise."

In her role as minister's wife, she writes booklets to educate women and children about Christianity and the dangers of communism (see Appendix B, Sabotaging the Youth, p. 226). "Little books," she said. "People don't read big books. I like to get to the common person."

She also writes travel books and biographies of South Africa's missionaries. In one, she traces a Scottish missionary's life in the Transvaal north of Johannesburg, "which in those days was very wild, wild animals and tribes." (Today 65 percent of the world's chrome—used on missile tips and other strategic machines—comes from this area in the northern Transvaal.)

Mrs. Malan probably was glad I was an American and not British. Afrikaners identify with those Americans who tamed a country, broke from British rule, and developed an economy and life pattern that white South Africans imitate. Their ties are with the most conservative sectors of the United States and Europe, including American fundamentalist religious leaders. Mrs. Malan has entertained the head of the California-based Campus Crusades for Christ.

"We have this sense that God plans everything. Nothing happens without His willing it," she said. "There is a certain task for us in this country and until it is completed, we just have to stay here.

"Now the question is . . . why did God ever bring us here? Christianity started in North Africa. It was quite a glowing thing. But it just petered out. Every trace of it was lost except for the small remnant you find in the Coptic churches in Ethiopia and the north. Otherwise the flame was just extinguished. Yet God started a new Christian flame down in the south—right down at the southern tip. And you know, I often think He could have started that anywhere— in the Congo, in Gabon. Why right down at the southern point? I'm not quite clear on that, but anyway . . . we have this sense . . . we have to stay here.

"This is why you find the English people leaving. I mean we could also leave. We've got lots of friends overseas. There are a few countries we love and we could be quite happy there. But we are going to stay here to the very last. Now people think that is very stubborn of the Afrikaner, but it's not really stubbornness. It is realizing that God is in control.

"You know it's a miracle, really. In our struggle with the British who wanted to take over this country, 260,000 women and children were killed in the first concentration camps they ever had in world history.

"After the Boer War there was nothing," she said. "The farms had been burnt down; everyone went back to his farm and found ruins and had to build from there. They were so poor, so very poor. The Afrikaner came through that period. So we Afrikaners look at everything that happens in world history and in our country's history as being part of the plan of God."

"What does the Afrikaner mean when he says he is born again?" I asked. (Mrs. Malan subscribes to the charismatic or evangelical movement although not all Dutch Reformed members do.)

"Being born again is not a feeling, it's a certainty; it's a sureness of where you are going, why we're all on earth. It's a certainty of where it all comes from, what God's plan is for you. Do you believe in God? A creator? Now, do you believe that Jesus is God's son?"

"Don't Christians believe we are all God's children?" I asked.

"Well, if you believe that, then you believe that Jesus is the greatest liar that ever lived! He said he came to save a lost sinner and make him the child of God. But if all people are the children of God, there is no need for Jesus to come to earth."

"Do you mean you are the child of God but other people are not?"

"No, by God's grace, I've been saved. It is to me the biggest miracle on earth," Mrs. Malan replied.

"Is, say, the person over there not saved?"

"I'm praying for him," she said. "And I'm saying, 'God, I cannot understand why some people have to be eighty years old before they see this light.'"

Mrs. Malan had just returned from three weeks' travel with one hundred young people. They had gone into the veldt to do "Christian work. We're very interested in reaching people when they are fairly young. We want them to form a group with a real sense of dedication."

She believes the division of people into groups is God's way of averting human conflict.

"The Bible says, 'the nations and the languages.' So though we would like one big world, with a world language, this will never happen because it's not according to God's biblical prophecy. For a Zulu to be proud of his Zulu language, his Zulu culture, is ordained by God.

"I don't think there is a division between Italian and Spaniard. These are countries. This is exactly how I see the future of South Africa (with black countries based on the tribes and one white South Africa).

"Apartheid is a geographical necessity because of city life and the way we're living today. I wouldn't make too much of the differences."

"Why is it that whites have 87 percent of the land when they are only one-seventh of the population?" I asked.

"But the natives have got the best areas in the country, my dear. Have you been down to the Transkei? Zululand? Some of the most beautiful land . . . but they're not developing it. They do not want to farm. They want to have clerical jobs.

"This has been proven in the whole of Africa. Why do you think the country of Malawi is such a success? Because President [Hastings] Banda has a vision that these people must be fed. The most important thing is food and he has developed a pride in agriculture. My husband has just been there. He went twice last year, and met Banda at the airport.

"You see, you must develop a pride in your soil. Do you know that South Africa is one of the greatest exporters of food in Africa?

"It is very difficult to live in a country like this with many racial groups. Britain is finding it difficult with their influx of Pakistanis;

Holland is finding it very difficult with the Moluccans and other groups. Yet, here, we have many different groups, eight or nine, with different languages. So this is very complex."

"Why doesn't the Afrikaner government divide whites the way it subdivided blacks?" I asked. "Why does the written law apply to blacks when there is none for whites?"

"Out of necessity," she replied. "In Europe, the British have England; the Welsh have Wales. If you live in Britain, you obey the rules of Britain. You've got to have a visa, a working permit. It was only in 1948 that separate development (the term whites now use for apartheid) was written into the law books. That was perhaps a pity. I believe in separate development. My question is whether it is still necessary to make it all law, since this country has three hundred years of natural division?

"The trouble is, of course, the city. I see this whole policy of separate development as an excellent policy. But now you find people moving out of the rural areas, coming to the big cities to work, and you have to accommodate them.

"The best would be to do what they do in Japan—move people with bullet trains into the (white) working areas by day and take them back to their homes at night (in the tribal homelands). I don't see why this country can't do it; we've got the money. But, of course, this is a large country, so it would be more difficult. But this would be the ideal thing."

Mrs. Malan told me she prayed for the leaders of the black homelands, which apartheid has declared "independent countries." "I know it is not an easy path for them, they've got the whole world against them, too, these poor independent people like the Transkei dwellers. They are not gaining world recognition. I pray for those men by name. It's such a terrific experiment. Without God, how could it ever succeed?

"I often think, God, why on earth did you put us here? I mean, we could have been in Los Angeles enjoying the sunshine!"

"Whites have a good life in this country," I said.

"The States have it. Look at your own country."

"Most Americans don't have servants," I said.

"Yes, but you've got all the electric equipment. Let me tell you, a lot of white women here are doing just that. They don't want native labor any more."

"What is the current wage for a servant in Northcliff?"

"About 50 or 60 rands," Mrs. Malan said.

"What do you pay yours?"

"About 50. We have one. She comes from the farm. Actually we brought her with us. We know her mother, father, and brothers."

"Where does she come from?"

"Near Brits. That's actually Bophuthatswana."

"What do you mean 'about 50 rands'?" I asked.

"Well, she gets about 48 [$54.20] a month."

"And she lives here?" I asked.

"She lives in our home. She has a bathroom."

"And you pay for food?"

"Yes, and she has a little girl on the farm, which to me, again . . . I have a little girl of seven; my last baby; my three sons have all grown up. I feel very sorry about my child growing up in the city. I would prefer her to be out in the Brits area."

"Would you like her to be there without you?"

"That's where the problem comes . . . but my girl could work in Brits. She wants to work here."

"Could she get as much money there?" I asked.

"No, but again, city life is much more expensive. Fifty percent of my community, and I'm a pastor's wife of a very affluent—this is one of the most affluent congregations in the country, so this isn't a common congregation—but I would say half have no domestic servants."

"Did you know the minimum wage suggested was 65 rands a month?" I asked.

"Yes. But we give her a lot of extras, you know."

"Have you ever asked if she'd rather have the money?"

"Yes. Often she's willing to come for 20 rands. And we pay for special needlework classes. I've given her a sewing machine; she's started the classes to learn how to make something for her daughter."

"Can her daughter come here?" I asked.

"She comes every holiday . . ."

" . . . to live with her mother?"

"It would be too far to travel to school. She can't speak a word of Afrikaans or English."

"Do you find it acceptable for a mother to be separated from her child?" I asked.

"Well, it is an illegitimate child. That child shouldn't have been," she replied.

"Do you think she loves her child less?"

"No, I don't say that. But now she's got a husband whom she will probably marry (legally). She will have to make a decision. A lot go back to the homeland. Actually, I would like that for her. When her homeland became independent and their new president was elected, I sent her home for the festivities. I would like her to go again. I don't suppose I will have her much longer."

I later learned that Rachel Pohlwani, Mrs. Malan's domestic servant for ten years, earned 42 rands a month and had not one, but four, children. Her major complaint was that she was not paid enough money. Initially Rachel Pohlwani agreed to an interview, but she changed her mind because her boyfriend told her not to talk to Kitty Duma, a woman interviewed later in this book.

"Will you get someone else if she leaves?" I asked Mrs. Malan.

"No, I won't. My boys are grown and leaving home."

"Will you get a char to come in several times a week?"

"Yes," Mrs. Malan said. "But you don't know the personal relationship that exists with my girl . . . the love that can exist, the love between me and this girl. Her mother whom I know, her sister, her little brothers who visit and talk about what they study. You don't know about this. And the little girl who comes to play lies on my lounge, looks at TV with my little daughter, and goes to her room. They sit and eat mielie pap on the floor. You don't know this. You haven't been living in this country long enough."

Mrs. Malan stopped to pour some tea.

Did she think life in South Africa had undergone many changes? I asked.

"Let me tell you, the National Party has moved in the past thirty years," she replied. "If you said to an Afrikaner in 1948, we'd be having separate bantustans or homelands, or states . . ."

"But wasn't that always the central aspect of apartheid?" I said.

"A few leaders had the idea of bantustans, but not the common crowd. The people who were doing the voting had no idea. Now that we've given independence to Transkei, a lot of people are saying: 'Now look what you're doing! It's not going to work; now you're going to give Bophuthatswana its freedom."

(Gatsha Buthelezi, chief of the Zulus, South Africa's largest tribe, with five million people, heads the Kwa Zulu homeland. However, he has refused "independence." Because he works within the apartheid system, the Afrikaners have considered the creation of an equivalent but different status for him.)

"People are saying," Mrs. Malan continued, " 'What mess have you got us into? Whites should have just kept the control.' "

To Mrs. Malan, apartheid means that every nation (tribe) is being developed to its full potential. "That is not happening in the United States," she said, "which is why you are having a lot of trouble."

"Do you think apartheid is wrong in any particular areas?" I asked.

"No, no. Because people want to be with their own people. We find it here."

"But if people in South Africa don't communicate with each other, don't you run the risk of war?" I asked.

"I'm very keen on the Afrikaner going out to have contact with the black," she said. "You say, now why don't we meet up with blacks? But we hardly meet the English-speaking whites, you know what I mean? So, to us, it's not that abnormal."

"Do you believe American blacks should be sent to places like homelands?" I asked.

"They have no land, those people," she replied. "They haven't got their own culture, their own language. There's nothing to be proud of. All right, they have to be Americans. I guess they have to be proud of that. But why did black power develop in the States? Did you ever think about that? Why did the television series "Roots" have the biggest viewing public in the States?

"Look, my mother was Irish. But my Afrikaans father and the Afrikaans language, it's part of my whole makeup. It's part of making me a person.

"Being a Spaniard in Spain and the Spanish language is what makes a person a real person. Yet in the States, what have you got? Black Americans who don't feel they belong to the right community and who are looking for their roots. Why is this?"

"But they do have a language and a culture," I said.

"But it's not their own. Why are they looking for their roots? Why did this cause such a stir in the States? Because every man wants to know where he is from. In Europe, they could have said, 'Let's just rule out all boundaries and be one conglomerate.' People aren't like that," she said.

"Would you like to be a black in South Africa?" I asked.

She hesitated. "I've never really thought about that. I've read Black Like Me, which was written in America. I thought, if I were to write a similar book in South Africa, how different would it be?" She paused, considered, then went on enthusiastically, "You know where I would like to be a black? In an independent black state like Bophuthatswana, electing my own black president, black cabinet. You know why? Because we Afrikaners have this feeling that we like to be with our own."

"Would you like to be black in Soweto?" I asked.

"I wouldn't. I wouldn't move to the city because I'm not keen on city life."

"But you live in the city."

"Because we have work to do in this congregation. I like the country better. If I were a black man I would not come to Soweto. A lot come thinking it's put together with gold, that the money's here. I suppose, in a way, it is. People don't realize when you move to a city, everything becomes more expensive: travel, clothes . . . so I wouldn't move to the city. I know a lot of blacks in rural areas. They have their own piece of ground which they can till. They can put in their mielies (corn) and pumpkin. I would go for that kind of life."

Actually, Mrs. Malan talks to more blacks than most Afrikaner women because she speaks English. The ones she speaks to are mostly black people who work within the apartheid system, such as the government-approved mayor of Soweto, who was originally elected with ninety-seven votes.

She is also a member of Kontak, a small Afrikaner women's organization. Mrs. Malan attends their occasional social and cultural evenings, which include a few blacks and more coloreds.

"Of course, in Kontak we meet a good slice of the community, all kinds," Mrs. Malan said. "We have had black power people."

"Black Consciousness people have been to meetings?" I asked.

"When I say black power people, I mean, well, people who say things that make me rise from my seat. I understand the black consciousness. It is like Afrikaner consciousness. I think in itself it is a good thing—if kept within bounds. I don't say black power is a good thing, because I know a lot of other elements have crept into it in the United States.

"In this country, the Communist Party was banned and went underground in 1950. Their leader, Bram Fischer, was an Afrikaner. I'm very interested in subversion in this country," she said. "Do you know that in 1949, Australia was on the verge of a takeover by communists? And I think in this country, we have been close to it at times and yet it has been revealed. We believe that is God-ordained.

"None of us thought ten years ago the communist takeover would be so imminent. My husband is chairman of an international Christian organization, "Open Doors." Being connected with that for so many years, we have become conscious of the communist threat, and the way they operate. They are anti-Christ, antireligious."

Like many whites in South Africa, Mrs. Malan considers people who oppose apartheid to be subversive. One of the prime targets of these whites' wrath is the local English-language press.

"We have knowledge of a subversive force in the English press for the past fifty years. Look, if you keep telling people every day in the newspaper that the government is outrageous, everybody will be saying it in a few months. Isn't that so?"

"Are you worried about the future?" I asked.

"I do believe we are moving toward a more just society. When I say just, I speak of the way one human being handles anyone who is different—English, Zulu, Tswana, Sotho, or whatever.

"In the process of this development, it is a pity that petty apartheid, as they call it these days . . . I would even go further and say the way in which some whites treat blacks, or work with them or handle them, is not right. I have no good word to say about that.

"Look, in South Africa, there will be as much trouble as there are outside agitators. That's what I want to say to you. I think there is discontent, but a lot is being done to normalize things. With all the outside influence, I think we might have trouble, yes. The few hotheads, like the Stokely Carmichaels, the Martin Luther Kings— those are the people you meet—the few intellectuals. Do you meet the ordinary black person? The common crowd in the bantustan?

"You know what we found in the United States? We found Americans had terrible guilt. It was so pronounced.

"You see, you Americans took people as slaves. You hounded the red Indians. You sent the cavalry against the Indians. You killed thousands. You killed all those buffalo. We didn't do that."

"What about the seven hundred black people who were killed during protests in 1976 and 1977 in South Africa?" I asked.

"And why did they riot? Why were there instigators? They want to take over. There'll be a revolution in England. France will fall. Italy's going to go. The Americans have lost their leadership in the world. The Russians are gaining very fast. It could be the End Time which God has ordained. But all over the world, not only in this country. I don't know how long."

Freda van Rooyen with her minister, Dr. Gert Swart, and his wife

6

The Kontak

Organization

People have to let us do it in our own way, our own time, even if they think we haven't got the time. If outsiders continuously pressure us, it makes the Afrikaner aggressive. He turns and walks back a few paces instead of forward. I think there's too much interference.
—*Freda Van Rooyen, 1979*

Three weeks after Soweto made front-page news overseas in June 1976, an Afrikaner newspaper reported a new women's organization, Kontak, founded by thirty-four-year-old Freda Van Rooyen. I first met Freda in July 1976, almost a year before I met Thenjie. I interviewed her again extensively in late 1978, shortly after Thenjie was sent to prison for the fifth time.

Kontak intended to liberalize the conservative Afrikaner woman; but it also wanted to improve the image of the Afrikaner.

There remains disagreement among *verligte* (more adaptive) and *verkrampte* (hard-line) Afrikaners about how to do this. *Verkrampte* Afrikaners believe even the smallest concession to blacks will signify weakness. Kontak's unstated premise is: If Afrikaners would adapt to some degree to black pressure, an explosion might be prevented. Despite Kontak's goals, its founder, Freda, who is a *verligte* Afrikaner, insists Kontak is not a political organization.

I interviewed Freda in her suburban Randburg home, which, like the Malans', displays a family crest. A new sand-colored adobe house with a central plant-filled patio, it was designed by Freda's brother and is worth 70,000 rands ($80,500). Freda's husband, Ewdie, is a dentist who began his career in Potchefstroom. Their annual income is between 30 and 36 thousand rands ($34–$41,000).

Freda readily admits that not everyone would want a house with so many windows and a cocoa-colored, barrel-shaped bathtub in the master bedroom, but it suits her style fine.

"Freda likes to think that she is rich, but she just associates with the Afrikaners who are," a friend of hers said.

Freda is an active hostess. Her home is an open, friendly one with numerous pets and with people dropping by. In the midst of it all Freda studies for a master's degree in medical sociology by correspondence course from the University of South Africa in Pretoria. She has her B.A. in social work from the University of Pretoria.

"Let's face it" is Freda's trademark phrase. She sprinkles "let's face its" throughout her bubbly talk, and her face is expressive beneath her short, curly, blond hair. I held several interviews with her over a two-month period and what follows was culled from those talks.

"Let's face it, it's a vast, vast task," she sighs, speaking of the intention of Kontak to change attitudes about Afrikaners. She never admits outright that it is Afrikaners' attitudes she must change, too. The difficulty is that she thinks she must make these changes without admitting that Afrikaners' present attitudes are wrong. The fear of a right-wing attack on Kontak makes her an adept backpedaler in conversation. (See Appendix B, Organizations Queried, p. 240)

By 1980 Kontak claimed a nationwide membership of five hundred women. In July 1976, Kontak's national council consisted of twelve Afrikaner women. It aimed to have "other colors" on the council after an election. There were one hundred white members in Johannesburg and small units had been organized around the country. In 1978, a colored branch was begun with fifty members. No black branch existed in Soweto, although fifty members were tentatively organized in Alexandra, a small black area right in the middle of Johannesburg.

The Broederbond stamped its approval on Kontak as quietly as a watermark. Both Dr. Gerrit Viljoen, chairman of the Broederbond at the time, and Dr. Willem de Klerk, a top Broeder and editor of *Die Transvaaler* newspaper, were on Kontak's all-male advisory board.

Nevertheless, attacks on Kontak from the right, especially by wives of cabinet ministers, did more to label Kontak "liberal" than did its philosophy.

"We are fighting a battle, trying to change the image black people have of the Afrikaner," Freda said. "If we want to change the situation in South Africa, this image must be changed. Look, you must accept the government and try to work within.

"I believe next year we will make an impact. I started a project for this year, a musical evening in the civic center, with the Soweto

Youth Orchestra and our white youth orchestra. Things like that will make the public sit up and take notice. We had an Afrikaans prose evening. It was fantastic. These people never listened to Afrikaans the way they did that evening. To them it was one of the most fulfilling experiences.

"And the visit to Soweto was the most exhilarating experience I've had in the past two years. We went to a swimming pool. We saw the children really enjoy swimming. My friend said, 'You know, for the first time in my life, I have the feeling it must be nice and enjoyable to be poor.'

"The black youth club in Soweto wanted to do something for us. The competitors in a body-building contest performed. It was hilarious. A little boy of three, no ruddy muscles, only tummy, suddenly pulled in his tum and there was nothing. He had a huge chest and was making muscles with those thin little arms. It was unbelievable. The children thoroughly enjoyed what they were doing."

She spoke of the Kontak achievement in the township of Alexandra, a one-mile-square black slum, festering amidst white Johannesburg suburbs. Freda claimed that as a result of a Kontak memo, the government deferred plans to remove black families from Alexandra, which had been designated an area exclusively for migrant workers without families in the city. However, the government continued to build huge dormitories for the migrants in the township even as Freda spoke.

Like most Afrikaners, Freda has not read what black leaders like Steve Biko have written.

"Our experience is with the ordinary people more than with the leaders," she said. "That is important. You find ordinary people have a difference with leaders. It's the simple, day-to-day man who is seldom quoted.

"We try to get the black newspaper as often as possible. Rosie (her domestic servant) and I share a paper. You find a lot in there. I have read everything Percy Qoboza has written. His articles were quite in depth." Qoboza was detained for five months in 1977 and his newspaper, *The World*, was banned. He started another, *The Post*, with continued sponsorship from a white corporation, the Argus Company. *The Sowetan* has since replaced *The Post* and Mr. Qoboza is no longer editor.

"That's given us a fairly good insight into what black people feel. I've done a lot of reading on Africa and South Africa. Biko I've never read. He and the Black Consciousness people severed all links with the white community. You know, I don't think Afrikaners realized it at the time. They thought he was pushing away from the

English-speaking liberals and might join hands with the Afrikaner people."

"What about the police actions?" I asked. "This must negate whatever trust Kontak develops. The blacks hate the Afrikaner police," I said.

"I was thinking of a group of youngsters I met the other day," Freda said. "They said the police have helped them a lot to find people. I'm thinking of a black woman who lost her son for a fortnight. Apparently he went to football and when he came out he was attacked by tsotsis (hoodlums). He was in such a state they left him for dead. The police picked him up, took him to a hospital, but he had nothing to identify him. He couldn't speak because he had a broken jaw. The mother went from police station to mortuary to hospital and nowhere could she find him. She said the way the police helped her is unbelievable. They went to a mortuary and opened sixty-five coffins to find her son. So, don't be unfair to our black people. They don't generalize about not liking the police. I wish you could sit in on discussions we've had with black people. We have come to the stage where we are brutally frank with one another.

"For instance, the home [cottage] industries that we want to start in Soweto. This black man phoned us. He said, 'Look, there are many out-of-work people in Soweto. The situation is getting worse. We as a group feel we've got to start doing something, but we haven't got the knowledge on our own. Would you help us?'

"So we said, 'Come to us and let's talk about it.' He brought the products made at home and said, 'Please evaluate. Which things will sell? We want criticism.' We had a very frank discussion and sorted things out. After an hour-and-a-half meeting, I turned to the young man and said, 'Why? Why come to us? There are many English organizations, bigger and more efficient than we. Why come to us?'

"His response was, 'We know you will be completely honest with us. You have never tried to pacify us because we are black. You treat us exactly as you would treat your white neighbors.'

"That's exactly what I expect from the South African. We must be able to say to each other when we don't like what others are doing . . . not in a reproachful way, in a positive way.

"It is frustrating when you work with black people and they don't see things the way you do. They don't have the same tempo of work that you have; they don't realize what time is . . . that time means money and is important. Those are frustrations we've got to accept. In the beginning we used to arrange meetings with blacks. It killed me when we said, "Meet at ten" and they would dribble in about twelve o'clock. It makes it impossible for those really pressed for time to work with them. They've got to accept us if they want to get somewhere. By working together, sharing, being honest with them—I'm very straightforward with black people—I think one can really get far."

On another day, during a dinner party, Freda introduced two *verligte* couples—an Afrikaner minister and his wife, and an English-speaking South African Kentucky Fried Chicken executive and his Afrikaner wife.

Seated next to me, the Afrikaner minister, respected for his *verligte* credentials, muttered in hesitant English, "The country is a mess, such a mess, that only a revolution can clean it up." Earlier, however, he cautioned Freda not to risk talking to banned people while she was head of Kontak.

The businessman protested the ostracism of the English by the Afrikaners. He'd wanted to participate in Covenant Day celebrations but the Afrikaners made it an exclusive holiday. (Afrikaners believe they have a covenant with God to be in South Africa; and every year they celebrate their pioneer victory over the Zulus to remind them of this holy covenant.)

Freda claimed she was raised "to accept all people as people. However, in England, I realized it's very important to belong somewhere. Suddenly I started missing things I never thought were important: my church, my language, being able to turn around in a shop and speak to someone in Afrikaans. I missed going to a doctor and being able to explain what was wrong with me. The frustrations were unbelievable. What I learned in sociology about your group being important became real to me. Now, I feel what we as a group have, we must share with other people: our culture, our language, our literature.

"I can't see Afrikaans dying," Freda said. "It's not all that easy for a language to die anyway. Think of the Welsh language. Everybody thought it was dead and now suddenly it's reviving and people are starting to learn it again. It's a pity you can't read it," she told me, "because there really are fantastic things written in Afrikaans.

"I think Afrikaans is easier than English; it's a simpler form of using words. There's a lot of warmth in it. For instance, I was thinking of a little poem we read over the weekend in *Rapport*. Let me translate: 'The flowers at Christmas are rubbing their hands together like the Jewish people.' Now, you can imagine if in three or four words you can say that . . . and the flowers . . . you can imagine them sitting there just like a Jewish shopkeeper," Freda smiled. "It's fun.

And that is what is so wonderful about the language. There is such warmth and happiness and expressiveness."

Freda worries about how other whites view the Afrikaner group.

"I think we are defensive, yes. I think so. But we are attacked so often and called the oppressor. The Afrikaner tends to defend himself more than necessary, and by doing that we harm our image. If we could be as honest and self-critical publicly as we are among ourselves, people would have a better understanding of what we are really like. I feel it is a pity that people from outside can't hear how Afrikaners talk among themselves: how we face the issues. The way we have been attacked by the English press in South Africa isn't easy to accept. They make the Afrikaner defensive.

"It makes me sick . . . all the damn interference from outside. It makes our whole situation more difficult. We've got to waste millions of rands sorting out the image that the outside world has of us."

"Why not forget about what they think?" I asked.

"Well, you tell the government that. Or go and tell the American government, because if we don't spend money on our image, the next thing will be economic sanctions. And then our black people are going to suffer, and boy, are they going to suffer. I'm well prepared to suffer with them, but I know they will find it the hardest."

"But the world's criticism of the Afrikaner—doesn't that have more to do with the policy of apartheid?" I asked.

"Oh, the policy is part of it. Many of us feel we want to change but it is not easily done. It's a slow process and that's got to be accepted.

"People have to let us do it in our own way, our own time, even if they think we haven't got the time. If outsiders continuously pressure us, it makes the Afrikaner aggressive. He turns and walks back a few paces instead of forward. I think there's too much interference.

"The moment the government thinks Kontak might be a pressure group, they will move against us. As long as they accept us, we have reasonable discussions and can point out what is not right. I can think of many instances when the government was only too open to change things once they realized it was wrong. More good can come from working within than from sitting outside. I think we've got the trust of the black people who know and work with us. We will always be honest about things. If we come upon something where there is gross discrimination, where things can be changed from within, we will do our utmost.

"We want to do away with the aggressiveness of one group toward another. Once the ball starts rolling, people will realize we don't need laws to keep us apart. We don't need to fear each other. I think the whole attitude of the white people would be more lenient. They would open up. They would force the government to change.

"I know about the Afrikaner. It's no good getting up to shout. He won't listen to you."

"Would you consider this a Christian government?" I asked.

"That's a difficult question," Freda said. "Often people truly believe the things they do are right; they even see in the Bible reason for what they do. But maybe their whole explanation, their whole way of seeing the Bible, could be wrong.

"Those people will give reckoning once they get up there (after they die). It's not something I can do anything about."

"A black woman told me Afrikaners are not Christians," I said.

"I disagree with this woman. I would like to meet her. She makes the statement cover all Christian Afrikaners. I'm sorry, it shows she does not know that many, not intimately."

"Isn't it the design of apartheid that she not?" I asked.

"Up to this stage, yes," Freda replied. "More and more people from white areas are trying to reach out to black people. It's getting better every day—I honestly believe that.

"My question to her, if I ever met her, would be: How can black people be Christian if they are, you know, doing violence, not only to us, but against their own people—you know, things that worry me and scare me. Dishonesty. But I cannot judge all black people because of a few examples. You know, in sociology, we point out how dangerous it can be to generalize about a whole group of people. I think we have many examples of Christian Afrikaners coming out and opposing apartheid," she said, then invited me to talk with her minister.

"Whatever he says, that's what I believe," Freda said.

Her church in Johannesburg is the Andrew Murray congregation. It sits back to back with another Dutch Reformed Church, which would never allow a black to walk into its services.

Freda's dominee, Dr. Gert Swart, is *verligte*. In his church, blacks are occasionally guest preachers.

"Ten years ago it was unthinkable to come into a Dutch Reformed Church without a hat," Dr. Swart said one Sunday in an interview with Freda present. "At the 1978 synod—on my motion— we pushed and won. Hats are no longer required."

Dominee Swart's congregation is made up of English-, German-, and Portuguese-speaking people as well as Afrikaners. "Often it's people of (religiously) mixed marriages who must find somewhere to go," Freda said.

Dr. Swart's sermons are in English. That day his sermon focused on the question, Is the Afrikaner a Christian?—a topic obviously prompted by my previous question to Freda. He spoke of a Japanese man, converted to Christianity, who could not believe Westerners were Christian because they dropped the atomic bomb on Hiroshima; of an Indian Christian convinced that Englishmen could not be Christian because they stole thousands of diamonds from the bathroom of an Indian palace and replaced them with tiny mirrors.

After the sermon, Dominee Swart elaborated to me in his apartment in the church edifice. Freda was in the background talking to his wife.

"The moment you say 'the Afrikaners' you are generalizing. You could say Zulus or Americans. The Bible shows us there are no Christian people on this earth. The Afrikaners are not a Christian people, but neither are the Americans.

"We have our cultural identities; we have ethnicity. You cannot deny ethnicity, not in the United States," he insisted.

"I talked to a lot of blacks in the United States. They said, 'Give us Texas; we want our own state.' That was an idea they had.

"Ethnicity is a fact. I don't like the fact. I will never say that God created ethnicity. But it was the will of God that it happen."

"Should an entire system of government be based on ethnicity?" I asked.

"Ethnicity is a fact of human life. It is not law. What is wrong in South Africa is, the government tried to be the guardian of ethnicity and, in the process, they hurt a lot of people."

"But the government in South Africa claims to be a Christian government," I said. "Are you saying they cannot make that claim?"

"Ya, no, all right, the government claims to be Christian. I think with the knowledge they have, they are honest to think they are Christian. When I was a young boy, they always compared the Afrikaner to the people of Israel," Dominee Swart recalled. "We grew up drinking that in with our mother's milk. But things went wrong: we started to twist the Bible to suit our views. But so have the Americans," he said.

"Shouldn't one fight a system one disagrees with?" I asked.

"You must fight in such a way that you do not alienate yourself from your people. I've got a very good friend, Beyers Naudé, who completely alienated himself," Dr. Swart said.

The dominee defended then–Prime Minister John Vorster, claiming he had much improved South Africa since the days of Prime Minister Hendrick Verwoerd. The point of the practical politician is to remain in power, Dr. Swart claimed.

"What is the alternative at this moment? If the prime minister relinquishes power, he foresees a complete communist takeover like in Mozambique. And he would say, 'I've got two wrongs to choose between. I'll choose the better of the two: remain in power and keep the communists out.' "

Dr. Swart stated his strenuous opposition to the Broederbond. When the names of members were published in 1978, he found many of his staunchest friends belonged, although he had preached to them against joining the secret organization.

"In your sermon you spoke of molding Christian thought. Now the church does that, yet the church supports apartheid," I said.

"Ya, but you cannot say the church supports apartheid. You are wrong saying that."

"What about the synod?" I asked.

"The snyod is not the church. The synod is the superbody; it's the united nations.

"I have nothing against the mixing of races," he said, "but the mixing of races is not the salvation of mankind. I'd rather . . . and this is a terrible thing to say . . . I'd rather have my little Annalee marry a Christian black than a heathen white. She's fourteen now; she's near the age of doing something like that. I have nothing against it."

"She's not likely to, is she?" I said.

"Not in South Africa," he agreed. "All right, nowhere in the world, not even in America. It's not done. I've seen excellent mixed couples in the United States," he added. "They call themselves black, but they are not. They are half and half."

"Would Jesus have slaves? He would never support apartheid, would he?" I asked.

"Now, now, now," Dominee Swart admonished. "You're making an assumption. Did Jesus ever ask slave owners to let their slaves go? Did he ever condemn slavery? He never said a thing about slavery."

"Do you think he would approve of it?" I asked.

"It was a pattern in his time which was accepted. He never said a word against it. He approved it in the setting in which it was done in that time."

"So he might approve apartheid?"

"If he lived in the society in which it was rife, like ours, yes. He preached salvation from sin, number one, and I think he would, in a gentle way, try to tell people to improve race relations.

"When I was a little boy, I accepted apartheid without question. Today I feel apartheid is wrong, but I'm not willing to say whoever approves of apartheid is, not a Christian. I can never say that," he concluded.

"Do you support apartheid, Freda?" I asked at another time.

"I don't think I ever stated that I support apartheid."

"You support the homelands and influx control, which is apartheid," I said.

"Before the homelands started, I opposed it violently," Freda said. "Once it was there, I tried to find good in it. In discussion with some of the homeland leaders, I suddenly realized if these people were in a united South Africa, they might not have had the chance to express themselves, to develop themselves in a leadership capacity.

"You must try and make the best of a bad situation and work toward a better end," she said.

"Do you know Beyers Naudé?" I asked.

"Yes. I knew him very well as a student. I adored him. I saw him when he was a missionary in Vendaland, and just before he was banned. I admired him, but I feel that Beyers, being what he is, people misused him for their own ends.

"We had a black friend. She left to study in America. She said, 'Beyers Naudé is such a good man, but he doesn't realize people use him. He's so kindhearted and has given himself so much to what he believes, that he cannot see the wrong from the right.' "

"What kind of wrong?" I asked.

"I don't know. We didn't have time because she was on her way to America. She worked with him at the Christian Institute and said, looking in from outside, seeing how people misuse this man, she decided to leave. To her, it was a very upsetting thing.

"I met Beyers twice after he was banned," Freda said. "Last Christmas, just after church. He's allowed to go to church—not to ours, no, to another congregation; he is a member. And one day, about six months ago, at an auction, he was there.

"I spoke to him on both occasions," Freda said, "but not in any depth."

"Weren't you curious? Didn't you have any questions for him?"

"No, not really. I can see why he did it, out of frustration with what he sees wrong in our society.

"But to get emotional, to go out in the streets and get rid of your frustrations is much easier than the way Kontak has chosen. It's difficult to change attitudes that have prevailed for three and a quarter centuries. But I believe in perseverance. Look, you don't have to do it in an aggressive way; there are many, many ways of fighting."

"But Beyers was not aggressive," I said.

"Fine. But I think it wasn't the way Beyers said it; it was what he said. Maybe because he's so calm and so unemotional in the way he says things. It seems to make him more dangerous. Often it is the calm, detached people who are the most dangerous."

"Was he influencing people?"

"Yes, I'm positive. It's why they worried about him. But not to worry. Beyers still has a long way to go. He's still doing his share."

"How do you compare South Africa's security laws with those of other countries?" I asked.

"I haven't lived in the Soviet Union," Freda said. "One hears things, but you often wonder if it's the full truth. No, I wouldn't call South Africa a dictatorship like the Soviet Union. We tend to make use of some of their methods, but also some of those used in Africa. Because, let's face it, we are part of Africa. This is something that happens in Africa. People are often banned without knowing why. Even worse, they are killed.

"Some of the cases are terrible. I would prefer people taken to court and given a chance to defend themselves. I don't like detention without a hearing; awful things can happen to people now.

"On the other hand, if the safety of the state is in question, must it make everything known, must it take these people to court? Isn't it truly a safety measure?"

"Wasn't that the attitude under Hitler? And that later, people said they didn't know what was going on?"

"Maybe you misunderstood me," Freda said. "When I know a person has been detained unnecessarily, I don't think we (Kontak) would let it lie. In Germany, the people just ignored it. I think we are doing our share."

"Wasn't the Black Consciousness medical clinic near King William's Town an excellent community project? Why would the government eliminate it?" I asked.

"Maybe they really had a reason. If it was a completely open, serious project, it's a terrible pity it happened. If they were using it—with the aid of white people—as a front to work against the government, to work for a kind of revolution, then they got what they deserved.

"It's difficult to express an opinion about (Black Consciousness) people I have never met."

"Did you try to meet some?"

"We've met some of them. I can't remember the names. I was still with Women for Peace. A group came out and met with us. Dr. Ntatho Motlana, who is not with Black Consciousness, but he sympathizes. If Biko was aboveboard, I will never condone what happened to him. It was terrible.

"But the other thing is to get proof. Now let me tell you what happened to us. We were told by (Anglican Bishop) Desmond Tutu about people who were tortured. I said to him, 'For God's sake, do me a favor: bring the people to me and show me,' because he said they were still wounded.

" 'Please bring them to us.' You can never say to people, 'I have heard that has happened to someone.' They won't believe you. But if you can say, 'I've seen it with my own eyes,' then you've got something to work on. But hearsay is never any good.

"I said to Desmond Tutu, 'If you can, take them in your car to (Minister of Police) Jimmy Kruger and show him.' (To blacks, Kruger is most detested. In his double post at the time as Minister of Justice and Police, he approved detentions and signed banning orders.)

"Look, I would never accept torture. Maybe that is where I differ from other people. As a physiotherapist, I worked in a hospital and I saw what black people did to other people. When that happens, the rest of the world says nothing. But the moment a white person does that to a black person, then it's sin.

"You know, I wish you could meet my friend. Six weeks ago, her mother was sitting in the kitchen minding her own business. A black man came in and attacked her. The most brutal attack one can think of. That will never reach the overseas press. If a black man can do it to a white, there's no harm done. And that is the unfairness of the whole situation."

"There were many eyewitness reports," I said, "of blacks being shot by police in Soweto. There are names and addresses of people killed . . ."

"How many people were killed by actual police fire?" Freda asked. "Very few from the weapons the police used. The state pathologist and I had a long, long discussion. The sorry part is that people were shot by police, but other people started shooting, too. Where they got firearms from nobody knows.

"They used them against their own people. What makes it so terrible is people would turn round and say, 'Six hundred were shot by the South African police.' That wasn't the truth. There's another side. The pathologist said lots were shot by the police. Others were dragooned. Others were shot by strange weapons the police never, ever, used. He could give proof. He had documents.

"The pamphlets found in Soweto telling how to make petrol bombs were obviously done by a group from the outside, radical people trying to undermine the whole social situation in South Africa. We don't need that.

"We've had marvelous experiences where black people came to

us (Kontak) and said, 'They're out looking for us.' I said, 'I'll make inquiries. You phone me back.' When he does, I tell him, 'You can go home; everything is straightened out.' I'm often in contact with the previous head of security police, General Michael Geldenhuys. That is what makes Kontak meaningful. We've got open doors to the police and to the government. We can sort out things."

I asked Freda what she thought the future would bring. In her view, South Africa will eventually become a loose constellation of black and white states—which is the current Broederbond plan. In a confederation whites would hold economic control.

"We will be able to share, but on what basis is difficult to know now," Freda said. "That's got to be worked out by experts. But, let's face it, we have to think of *now* and do whatever we can *now* and try not to think what the future will be like.

"To be quite honest with you, the people I'm interested in are the ones who still try to sort out the problems of South Africa, try their level best to be fair in the situation—which is often difficult. Those people realize if black people in South Africa take over, it's going to be dark chaos. There are many black people who realize that."

Christelle
Marais

Susann Wessels, her arm bandaged after a dog bite

7

Women

Who Say

They Know

You see, the black man has a different idea of violence. It does not mean that much. It's not as moral a thing as it is for whites. Human life, or life in general, does not mean that much, or does not have the same value to them that it has to a white man. —*Christelle Marais, 1978*

O ne warm summer day in December I drove to the wealthy Johannesburg suburb of Houghton to tape an interview Freda set up with herself, Christelle Marais, and Susann Wessels. All were members of Kontak.

Christelle Marais's husband, Kowie Marais, left the Broederbond, joined the Progressive Federal Party (PFP), and became a member of Parliament. He did not go so far in opposing apartheid as Beyers Naudé and was, therefore, not as ostracized by Afrikaners.

Susann Wessels, a delicate and elegant woman, is married to a rich industrialist who also owns an apartment in Paris that she visits regularly. She was older than both Freda and Christelle, who were in their late thirties. We met at Susann's house, a white rectangular-faced mansion, high on a hill and with a magnificent view.

We settled ourselves over cups of coffee in the unpretentious, friendly manner Afrikaners have with American whites. The elegant living room was lined with South Africa's unique, expensive yellow-wood. A light-brown dog, a Weimaraner, with eerie turquoise eyes, sat like oriental statuary at the end of one sofa. After talking a few minutes, Susann tried to coax the huge animal out of the living room. He growled and sank his teeth into her arm, slicing to the bone. In an alarmed but efficient flurry, Freda drove Susann to the doctor for stitches after warning Christelle not to discuss PFP politics with me because "Kontak is not political."

Christelle did just that. In the early 1960s she thought apartheid was the final solution to South Africa's problems, but gradually she became disenchanted. Now she believes the PFP can serve as a catalyst to bring about peaceful change. She believes she has rejected apartheid, but she cannot imagine South Africa without influx control (pass laws). "You cannot just open the portals of the cities and sit back and watch people stream in."

She believes tribalism gives a black man his identity and she related an incident with Reverend Simeon Nkoane, whom she met at a party. She had said to him, "I notice some of your tribal traditions either going by the board or being westernized." "This man took me up very seriously and said, 'Who are you to tell us what we shall keep? We will decide for ourselves.' You know, I ended up apologizing most sincerely, I felt so bad. I had no intention of insulting him. I meant it as a compliment."

I asked Christelle why cabinet ministers were forced to resign over money scandals but not over the more than six hundred blacks killed.

"Six hundred people killed? Where? Do you mean during the riots?" she asked.

"Why don't whites know how many blacks were killed?" I asked.

"I think the public is not well informed. I don't know whether you are aware that this was not published in our newspapers," she said.

"But I read it there," I said.

"Was it the English newspapers?" Christelle asked. "All whites don't read the English papers. Very few of them read any newspaper at all. The ordinary man in the street is not politically minded. He has a hazy idea of what the riots were all about. It's seen as a vast thing organized by the communists.

"We imagine there are three communists sitting behind every little bush. I'm not running this down; it is a vital thing. And if you look at what is happening in the rest of Africa . . . I would not accept communism," she said.

"What is communism in your thinking?" I asked.

"I basically . . . you see, that's the problem—we are afraid of communism, but very few of us can recognize it.

"To me, it's probably a question of economics. Communism is a way of raising people out of ghastly circumstances, as it was envisaged originally. I suppose there's something to be said for that.

"But the methods applied—I would not like to live under such a system. Also, it is antireligious. I am a member of the Dutch Reformed Church. I'm not a particularly religious person, but the golden rule, the suggestion of doing unto others as you want to be done by, that is how the church affects me."

Christelle noted "endless talks on communism over radio and television."

"Would you like to be black in South Africa?" I asked.

"As it is now? No, definitely not."

"Are whites afraid of blacks?"

"Yes, I think so, because there is a large percentage of violence among black people. You see, the black man has a different idea of violence. It does not mean that much. It's not as moral a thing as it is for whites. Human life, or life in general, does not mean that much, or does not have the same value to them that it has to a white man."

Christelle admitted, however, that even more than communism, whites are terrified of being "swamped by the blacks, that blacks will take power, that the white man will land between two warring black factions, and God knows what will happen to him then.

"If nothing else, these riots have made whites a bit more courteous toward blacks."

She was referring to such things as whites being made aware that black men do not like to be called "boy."

When Freda and Susann returned from the doctor, Susann's arm was bandaged. She insisted she was fine, and reentered the conversation with vigor.

"Would you like to be black in South Africa?" I repeated the question.

"No, of course not," Susann said vehemently. "I'm happy. I like the way I am, and I'm sorry for them, too. After all, I have merged further in civilization. It's a fact. I think I used the wrong word there . . . development. It's not that their development is so low; it was good; it was highly organized and good. It just doesn't fit in with the modern society we have which will be the dominant one, the white, as far as I can foresee."

"Do whites exploit blacks?"

"Are you thinking of industry?" Susann asked. "They are not exploiting blacks, definitely not. They pay as much as they are worth. Look, there isn't a single word in our labor laws that says blacks must be paid less, not one, you can read it."

"But they are paid less, aren't they?" I said.

"The ones that become foremen and floor managers get the same salaries as whites. You know, the mines now pay more; the workers get a lot of other perks. In Europe, the miner wouldn't be housed."

"Migrant black miners are kept in all-male hostels. Is that why they hate to mine so much?" I asked.

"The miners aren't discontented," Susann said. "I often see them because we hire fifteen miners to work in our garden three or four times a year. They are picked at random. They like to come out and work on a Saturday, all perfectly happy. It's a great adventure for the black man to come here from the mines.

"My husband's textile factory was the first to use black labor. They had to train people who had never touched a machine. Actually, there's a very efficient section of the Department of Labor where any complaint is followed up and I know the inspectors there—they do follow up."

"Have you ever imagined yourself black?" I asked.

"I think every South African has, because we see them all the time," Susann replied. "South Africans didn't really look at black people for a long time. Now there are so many, we've become aware of them, naturally.

"It's marvelous the way they educate their babies. It's absolutely beautiful. The many languages they pick up, their faithfulness. Really, one's house servants, unless you're horrible, they are always faithful," Susann said.

"One of the problems they have at university is they start off fairly well and suddenly they fade into the background," Christelle said, adding it was difficult to study in Soweto's conditions. "You see, if you have a man who comes from a kraal [rural hut] and you put him into a university, can you imagine what kind of an adjustment that is?"

Susann concurred. "Unfortunately there's an apparent discrepancy. Africans have wonderful memories, but when it comes to thinking, the interpretative, the logical, that's difficult."

Freda agreed. "One day in a discussion group," she said, "a black said, 'On page ten, paragraph so and so, this is written.' He quoted the whole damn thing. The other students were in hysterics. None of us knew what was on page ten. But the black couldn't grasp the concept of the whole thing."

"Freda, what about you? You must prefer your situation to a black's," I said.

"Often I wonder . . . I would pack up and go and live an ordinary life near to nature and get rid of all these frustrations. The fallacy of getting the vote and that's the end of all expectations in life—it's rubbish."

"Why not give up the vote if it's rubbish?" I asked.

"Many whites *have* given it up," Freda replied. "They have stopped voting."

"But their interests are still protected," I said. "Perhaps they feel they don't need to vote."

"Whose interests are protected?" Freda said.

"Whites'."

"Mine? No. I don't see it that way."

"You can't say the interests of blacks are not protected," Susann interjected.

"No, no, no," Freda agreed.

"But blacks have only 13 percent of the land. There are twenty million. If they had a vote they would change that," I said.

"Do you think they want that land? Do you think they want it when they are not using it?" Susann said.

"Yes, more than the vote, they must want the land," I said.

"They say they want it, but what will they do with it?" Susann asked.

"I don't think they want it," Freda said.

"What do you think they want? Why do you think they risk dying?" I asked. "How many have died in the last year?"

"I know exactly; I've got a list of their ages and so on. It's not so terribly many," Susann said. "Fact is, they did die. There were bad conditions and there was an uprising. But these speakers who say they want more land, are they prepared to go and farm it? Do you think they've thought that out themselves? Lucas Mangope (president of Bophuthatswana) says he wants more land. Of course he says he wants more land. He wants to consolidate.

"They say they want more land because it has been said to them so often. Mangope's got all the farms he wants. (Kaiser) Matanzima (president of Transkei) saw to it that when our state (South Africa) brought farms for them to use, he and his brother took them. They want land but the others don't.

"There are places where children are undernourished but they are not dying of starvation," Susann continued. "It comes from ignorance; they don't give babies enough water to drink, so babies get diseases and die."

"And you give them money to go and buy food," Freda said. "Yesterday I said to my girl, 'Here's money, go and buy yourself food.' I came back and I said, 'You need more money? How much did you spend?' No, she bought a Coke."

"They think white bread and Coke is wonderful food because they think we eat that," Susann seconded Freda. "You have starvation in parts of the Transkei every so often and that's where they put red mud on their faces. They're very backward."

"Do you ever feel guilty that you have so much?" I asked them.

"No, I refuse to feel guilty," Christelle said.

"So do I," Freda added.

"I would feel guilty if I did not try to change the situation, but I do not feel guilty that I, at this stage, am more privileged than they are," Christelle explained.

"Do you think you should be more privileged?"

"No, it just happens it is the kind of life I was born into."

"We work jolly hard for it," Freda said.

"Jesus says a rich man cannot enter the kingdom of heaven," I said.

Both Christelle and Susann were silent.

"Well, you know," Freda said, "I think we tend to interpret the Bible much too literally. There are stages of being rich, and if you are selfishly rich, that is wrong. I often feel black youth think what we have, we just get. They think the government gives it to us."

"They think we just walk into a bank and get money," Susann said.

"But isn't it an advantage to be white here?" I asked.

"It's a disadvantage as well," Freda said. "We pay the most tremendous income tax. We pay a profit tax. It costs us a packet. You see, I've got one guilt feeling: Four and a half million white people in South Africa have done too much for too long for the black people in this country. I don't think anywhere else white people, a minority group, have done so much for a majority group."

"Why is it that blacks don't like the system?" I asked. "The woman who cleans my building said one day, out of the blue, 'South Africa is a shit country.'"

"But she did it for an audience," Freda said. "She knows you aren't South African. They are told this day by day, that South Africa isn't a nice country. But once you get to the educated, developed people they love it here. Just let them leave South Africa and they yearn to come back. It's their country and they love it when they're outside it. This is what they are told to say to overseas visitors."

Freda continued: "I asked my girl the other day, 'Would you like to go anywhere else?' She said, 'No, it doesn't really worry me.'"

"You know, when I visit my Afrikaner friends, if their girl has problems, they try and help her," Freda said. "Fine, they can't all pay fantastic salaries, but isn't it better to earn something than to earn nothing? I try to be realistic—relationships between people are much more important than a specific salary."

"How do you feel about the Immorality and Mixed Marriages Act?" I asked.

"Why must we have a law?" said Freda, voicing the *verligte* position. "Very naturally people are against mixing. Black people are as scared as we are because it has been proven it seldom works."

"I would not agree with mixed marriages, make no mistake," Christelle said. "But it is each individual's right to make up his own mind. It's a normal human thing to mix with your own type."

Christelle called the Immorality Act a form of hypocrisy, citing the frequency with which it is contravened. "The Orange Free State has become notorious for the activities of some of its men, although it's a very small percentage."

"When we grew up," Susann said, "little girls were told to stay away from blacks because people were afraid."

"The nanny was nothing," Freda added, "but the black man . . ."

"Yeah, because, after all, we started here with blacks in an absolutely primitive state," Susann explained.

"And their sexual attitude is completely different," Freda said.

"They had diseases and so on," Susann added. "Even if your mother never actually said, 'Don't talk to a black man,' she would tell you in a subtle way. A lot of people had animosity toward the blacks. They were dirty; they were unpleasant, many of them. But many people have developed to a stage now where they can admire blacks and see that they're beautiful."

"Susann said they *had* diseases—they still have them and it is a tremendously serious situation," Freda said. "Blacks are born with gonorrhea and syphilis. Do you realize how serious that problem is? And people don't talk about it."

"There are still people who make a fuss because when a black servant registers he has to be seen by a doctor. We've been criticized for that!" Susann said. "It's a marvelous thing; they are treated. Of course, every time his contract is renewed, it's done again."

By contrast a black man had recently described to me the humiliation when, renewing his pass, the Afrikaner officials demanded he lower his pants for inspection. "Migrant workers," he added, "are lined up and examined like cattle."

Do these Afrikaner women find nothing wrong with apartheid?

Freda said, "Maybe we handed over too much to our church and our government and that made it authoritarian."

"Will it be possible to regain control?" I asked.

"That's the sixty-thousand-dollar question," Christelle said.

"I think so," Freda said, "if we really work at it—Susann?"

"Yes, I think so, if the demand for change becomes a little bit wider . . ."

These *verligte* Afrikaner women were friendly, like many other Afrikaners I met. They want to persuade other whites to be on their side. Their side—apartheid—has variously been renamed separate development and plural relations. *Verligte* Afrikaners believe their semantics. In the West, white businessmen want to believe them too. Upon them, General Motors, Ford, Chrysler, Leyland, Polaroid, IBM, and many others place their hopes for averting greater conflict. Yet the majority of people in South Africa—the blacks—are not paying attention to changes in the apartheid lexicon. They are no longer fooled by shifts in the language and they are engrossed, now, in listening to one another.

8

Heresies

I'm not an activist, or a liberalist. I'm just carrying on and
feeling guilty about it because I'm part of the setup.
—*Anonymous Afrikaner woman, 1978*

T hree or four times she said, "Why do you want to
interview me? I'm not anyone."

In fact, she was an unusual Afrikaner who
voiced heavy despair about "what my people are doing to the
blacks." Speaking with her in Durban, one felt white South Africa's
tragedy, its fatalism.

"I would say what I want if it weren't for my husband," she said.
"If I were single, I would do it. If I speak out, he will lose his job; they
will say we are communists. I can't speak out."

She agreed to be interviewed if she could remain anonymous.
We met for lunch in a cozy, candlelit restaurant that served small
grilled-in-butter lobsters from the Indian Ocean.

A large-boned woman with a mobile face and warm blue eyes,
she had been a social worker until the authorities decided her concern about the people was too deep; they ordered her to leave.

She and her husband talk freely with one other Afrikaner couple, but no one else can know the extent of her heresies.

Her experience was not with educated, literate blacks except for
the few "I came across in my efforts to assist the very needy—a
minister, a social worker here and there. I've moved with the outcasts, the homeless, the permitless people. I tried to assist them
because nobody else would. It's no use sending a black as an inter-
mediary because he simply can't reach the white official. I tried to
make life more livable for them because they really were so unhappy. Even educated blacks have to live in very awkward circumstances."

Her husband does not relate to blacks the way she does. However, she said, while she worked with blacks, he was sympathetic.
Now that she no longer does, she sees signs that he is retracting his

concern and becoming more conservative. That, she understands, too; for she is also desperately afraid.

"You know, I had a nightmare last night. A black terrorist in camouflage was standing over my bed. I was screaming. I woke up screaming. I nearly took my husband and bedclothes through the window."

She was worried about her teen-age son. "The other day I was out practicing shooting with him. I do it to try to develop a bond with him. While we were there, he said, 'A kaffir is a kaffir (nigger) and is born to be shot.' I was shocked, really shocked. But, you know, that is what young people are saying today."

A devoted Afrikaner, in love with her language, she sees that Afrikaner leaders have "feet of clay," and said true scholars must question deeply.

"We're a Calvinist church and we don't question its doctrines. Theological schools debate things up to a certain point. But only the theological faculty of the University of South Africa in Pretoria asks questions.

"Our Dutch Reformed Church is not in favor of the Masons, which is a secret organization. Therefore, I cannot accept the other secret organization, the Broederbond, and I won't. My husband is not a Broederbonder; he's not even a Rapportryer (the Afrikaner counterpart of Rotary and Lions). You have to be invited; you can't apply to it; you have to have connections.

"Other people don't mind the Broederbond; they say it is protecting Afrikaans culture and our language. But I don't think the language will be able to perpetuate itself. Only a small number in the world speak it. Lots of our people are becoming English speakers because they send their children to English schools.

"My son attended an English school for awhile. We were criticized for this. But many in our church congregation send their children, especially in this area; there are no Afrikaans schools.

"I accept this, but the Broederbond won't. I like the Afrikaans culture. The language is beautiful. It's the language I relate in. If I could speak it to you, I would say much more than I'm able to in English. It's a pity I can't use English better; I would like to.

"I wish, I really wish, you were able to read *The Traveling Years of Poppie Nongena*, a book by Elsa Joubert. It is one of the most wonderful experiences I've had in Afrikaans. She uses the language that the Xhosa Afrikaner speaks. It's not pure Afrikaans; it's a very queer sort of Afrikaans, but heartbreakingly beautiful. You can't believe . . . I get the shivers . . . I enjoyed the book so."

"What is it about?" I asked.

"This black woman travels between one pass office and the next, then to the homelands, never able to get a stamp to stay anywhere. I have never read such a disturbing book. I *know* what she went through, what thousands go through in our country. Most whites don't know.

"I'm not an activist, or a liberalist. I'm just carrying on and feeling guilty about it because I'm part of the setup.

"We feel so powerless. It's my people, I know; but I don't feel part of it. I'm unhappy; I'm frustrated. I want to be part of creating a new South Africa for everyone to live in but my hands are chopped off."

She wanted to hold onto her misery to remind herself of all that is done to black people by the Afrikaners.

"I feel guilty for my own people . . . what they do . . . the whole setup. I know how blacks feel. I know people like Poppie Nongena, struggling against permits and resettlement."

"Why do you care so much more than most Afrikaners?" I asked.

She spoke of her traditional Afrikaner upbringing with an authoritarian father, who was a policeman. "He was the station commander; everybody would listen to him. He's very rigid and has a very limited outlook, but because of his contacts with me, he knows more than most whites. He doesn't agree with my politics at all, not that I have politics. To me, it's just a question of human relations.

"I was about six years old when the Second World War broke out. My father joined the Osswabrandwag because he didn't want to fight the Nazis. He was transferred without notice about half a dozen times during the war. The pre-Nationalist government did not want him to settle anywhere. He identified with Germany, not because they were Nazis but because they were against England."

She never had servants and never mixed with blacks as a child. "But while I attended university, I took anthropology and visited the homelands on my holidays."

Her father was completely opposed to her obtaining a university education and forced her to take typing and bookkeeping. In part, she married to be able to go to the university level.

"After my studies, my first job with blacks was as a social worker in a hospital. I met hundreds of blacks. 'Madam, I have no house, can you help me? We're staying with other people. We're staying in a gutter. We're staying in a storm water pipe. We have no permit; we have no pass; help me.' I drove from office to office to office, to previous employers for records, trying to help them get a permit, a pass, a place to stay, pensions.

"When I moved into the hospital, the managing director of the

Bantu (African) affairs was an Afrikaner who couldn't understand how I could find a black woman beautiful.

"Many whites didn't understand how I could distinguish one black from another. They cannot, because they are not interested. When you regard blacks as human beings and are interested in them as individuals, you see they are different."

She described the Catch-22 legalisms that form the web of apartheid. She tried to assist a "chappie" who was born in the township. He met a farm girl from Excelsior, a town in the Orange Free State province, fell in love with, and married her. But the law did not allow the wife, whose pass book was for a rural "white" area, to live with him in the black urban area. To cohabit legally, the couple would have had to move to a tribal homeland, but they refused, since they had never seen the homeland. Now the man lives in the Kroonstad township, south of Johannesburg, and his wife visits him about once a month.

"They're people, they're people like you and me," she said. "Officials won't concede they are making enemies of people in our country. It's their country, too. We can't regiment people's lives like that. It's impossible."

She witnessed endless cases of injustice to blacks and recounted instances of corruption among Afrikaner officials in charge of the black urban areas.

"When I was working in the women's hostel I started a campaign about these women: married, divorced, unmarried mothers. All had to stay in hostels because of their jobs and remain separated from their children. I spoke to the officials time and again, until one day, an official told me, 'Look, if you want to do social work, get out of the hostel. You're here to supervise, not do social work.' So I left.

"Many of the women in the hostel should be home with their children. I wish you would be allowed into that hostel; you wouldn't sleep; you'd be too busy listening to the women's problems about children staying with strangers or old grannies; about giving exorbitant amounts of money, food, paraffin, and mielie meal to the old mamas who look after the children.

"And they are searching desperately for boarding schools to send their children to. Boarding schools are not allowed in the cities, and in the homelands there are no vacancies. A few years ago, the Dutch Reformed Church opened one in Bophuthatswana and there were more than four hundred applications for thirty-five beds.

"The whole policy is based on fear—the fear that Europeans will be pushed into the sea. You know, the whole of Africa is an example of what happens to whites. Here, they are determined to stay and they won't compromise.

"You see, in America blacks are one-tenth of the population and a basic fear of the white is always present there.

"This is our fatherland," she said. "We have no motherland to go back to. Ya, this country belongs to us. Our motherland was actually the Netherlands, mine was France. Now we're so intermingled we can't go back. This is our country; but I identify with the blacks in this country. I love my country and I love the blacks. I feel very endearing sometimes—I don't know how to express myself in English—an endearment for them and the position they find themselves in. You know, they've come a long way and they still have a long way to go to reach the level most whites have reached. And I'm really quite willing to pay tax and work and have a lower standard of living to accommodate them, to have all of us living in this country next to one another."

AMANDLA!
THE
TWENTY-ONE
MILLION

"Soweto, Soweto, Soweto": Train to Johannesburg, hostels for male migrant workers, and row after row of "matchbox" houses

9

Soweto,

Forbidden City

I t was always a relief after interviewing an Afrikaner to dip back into the other, larger world of South Africa, the black world—in this case, Soweto.

For most of the time I lived in South Africa I could not enter Soweto because it was closed off by police or was far too dangerous for a white. Johannesburg usually looks like a half-black, half-white city. Soweto is totally what apartheid intends—black, black, black, where whites stand out. Once inside friends' houses, however, there is no place more casually open to living.

Although I had not previously frequented Soweto much, in the last quarter of 1978 I could drive in with a permit from the authorities. Thenjie was in prison, but I could visit other friends, Thenjie's mother, and her cousin Thamie Coha. The layout of the city, whose name became known around the world, is dull and ugly, but its people are enormously attractive.

On June 16, 1976, Thenjie was in King William's Town with Steve Biko. But June 16 became a date she would honor the next year and the next for many years.

On that day, Soweto schoolchildren demonstrated peacefully against Afrikaans as the language used to teach in their schools. Police shot into their marching band and killed thirteen-year-old Hector Peterson. A journalist photographed the dead boy dangling in the arms of another young man; the boy's sister walked nearby, her face contorted, her hand flared in shock.

The government banned the photo. But it was too late. The impact on the black community was instant. The cry for *Amandla!* burst forth.

"They cannot stop our freedom. It is like the wild flowers. They can refuse to give a flower water and make the bloom less, but they cannot stop it."

The police tried. They used guns, dogs, helicopters, tear gas, and armor-plated vehicles. Students fought back with stones, gasoline bombs, and a hidden weapon: their knowledge of the Soweto terrain.

"The police can't find where the kids (student leaders) are sleeping at night and it's driving them crazy," said a Soweto professional man.

A few whites had been inside Soweto at the time of the protest and two were killed by students angered by the extreme police retaliation against their march. Afterward, the whites' image of Soweto as *swart gevaar* (black peril) solidified.

To whites, Soweto sounds like an African name, but it was not meant to be. The government assigned the name South Western Townships and, along the way, it was abbreviated to So-We-To.

Cut off and contained with only four entrances, Soweto sits like a thought shoved to the back of the mind. Without a permit on paper, a white cannot drive beyond the weathered warning signs at the fringe of the city. The authorities demand a reason for entering: a desire to look around is not enough. For that, a tourist bus is provided.

Soweto: Africans coddle the name in their palms, warm it up until it throbs, hum it back in their throats, roll it about on their tongues, and pronounce it "suh-*way*-too," like a Xhosa word that means "almost like our home."

In the evening Soweto traffic picks up. A nauseous, yellowish coal smoke drifts out from houses where suppers are cooking. The spun-glass smoke does not lift. People cough into its gauze.

Orlando's electricity power station is the largest construction in Soweto and lies halfway between Thenjie's house and her cousin Thamie Coha's. It looms through the soft coal smoke like a fairytale promising electricity so the people can live happily ever after. But the Orlando power plant lights up Johannesburg, not Soweto, where only 20 percent have electricity.

On moonless nights, most of Soweto is in total darkness. Homes such as Thamie's are lit with kerosene lamps and candles. Thenjie has electricity. But she has no bathroom and must bathe herself and Lumumba in a small enameled tin pan.

Whites with permits may fish and boat in the lake that adjoins the Orlando electric plant. A high fence prohibits blacks from entering. They fish a few miles away in the lake's overflow; they mill around in the marsh of tall, tasseled grasses. Men drag in their lines.

"God is good—sometimes they do catch a fish," Thamie said. There is no fish smell there, only the odor of grease and metal from a nearby levee where trains carry blacks to work in Johannesburg.

Soweto had one hotel, no pharmacy, one bakery, one supermarket. The South African government gains revenue by taxing beer and gas in the city. During the uprising, students gutted many government-built beer halls and ordered residents not to drink liquor on designated days in protest. Jagged burnt walls still stand. The government is building new beer halls constructed like forts.

In Soweto, there is little grass to clutch down the dust or soak up the rivulets of water. Thenjie's dirt yard and front road are typical and during rains can become virtually impassable. Unlike the lush Johannesburg gardens tended by blacks, most flowers in Soweto are wild. During March, as winter approaches, a flower, the cosmos, wavers over the fields. The petals, wine-colored or white, with seams like valentine folds, grow indiscriminately. They can even be seen around the dismal hostels of migrant workers who flow back and forth from city to countryside, their lives disrupted continuously by the forced repatriation to their homeland families.

The cosmos flowers waved in a sloping field of dry grass outside Gibson Thula's window. We were in his office fifteen miles north of Johannesburg in a black "location." He is the publicity secretary for Zulu Chief Gatsha Buthelezi's cultural organization, Inkatha.

Every year Thula arranges for Chief Buthelezi to visit Soweto and address the Zulu migrant workers living on the Reef around Johannesburg.

Migrant Zulus living miles and miles from their homelands come by the thousands to the Jabulani Soccer Stadium in the heart of Soweto. Most who come are middle-aged or older. Inside, Chief Buthelezi flicks his tribal stick amid the stamping Zulus, who swing knobkerries and sing.

People from the Black Consciousness Movement do not attend. They contend Chief Buthelezi reinforces apartheid by strengthening homeland ties with Zulus living in white urban areas; that he rallies them to concentrate on minor problems, diverting energy away from struggling for liberation. They insist he is not a national leader, as he claims, but a Zulu leader, advocating "Zulu Consciousness."

"When Gatsha gets angry, he says to people, 'I'm afraid of what the Zulus will do to you,'" Thenjie once said. "How can he be a leader, then, for all of us?"

"Soweto, Soweto, Soweto," go the simple lyrics of a popular song. The words repeat monotonously like the rows of houses that roll over the hills of the city. But the catchy tune is hard to forget. So, too, is the city. Its life flows from the people who survive despite police brutality, despite apartheid. Not a passive survival but a constant fight.

Winter and summer, ragged children play on unpaved streets in front of rows of tiny houses, which residents call matchboxes. A 1975 Market Research Africa Survey found 85 percent of the houses in townships had no bathrooms; two-thirds no hot running water; three-quarters were without ceilings.

The housing situation had not changed for the better by 1983 and more likely had become worse, since the government had not built houses to accommodate the burgeoning population. A *New York Times* report said it appeared the government had allowed fewer than 5,500 houses to be built in Soweto since 1970.

The actual number of people jammed into the township's 102,000 residences is at least 1.1 million and maybe 1.5 million. That's between 10 and 14.7 people per house and the houses are for the most part extremely small. The Urban Foundation says 32,000 houses need to be built just to house the existing population. The National Manpower Commission says that for the whole country, South Africa needs to build 560,000 more housing units just for blacks.

Thamie Coha lived in one room of a high-roofed, no-ceiling house. A narrow passageway led from the door to the stove at one side of the room. Every inch of space was utilized. Clothes under beds, suitcases on top of wardrobes, a small gasoline-run refrigerator, food staples in aluminum cans under a table next to the bright yellow "Ellis Deluxe" coal stove always kept hot for cooking; a portable radio, a kerosene lamp, and on the wall, two calendars from Fattis's liquor store. The toilet is in the back yard. Running water is drawn from a spigot on the side of the house.

Thamie, her eighty-year-old mother, her fifteen-year-old daughter, and her eleven-year-old son sleep on two beds and a cot. Their home is one room; other rooms in the same house contain other families.

Most South African blacks court a full house. They do not understand anyone choosing to live alone, as I did. They want to be with other people always, more than with books, television, or movies.

Unlike most Sowetans', Thenjie's personality has an unsettling lonely core that she seldom reveals, and which may come from an almost imperious sense of self-privacy. She has told few people the details of her life. Thamie says, "When Thenjie goes quiet, it is scary."

Usually she is quite the opposite. "I can't stand quiet company," she said. "I always feel obliged to speak. And I can mix in any company, from the doctors, who are supposed to be the highest in our community, to the street sweeper. With the old, the young, I mix fairly well. No, very well. I can play with kids Lumumba's age and I can mix with kids of nineteen and speak their language. I can talk the language of my mother's friends."

As they say in South Africa, " 'Strue, 'strue." I've seen her do it and 'strue. When a woman like that becomes politically conscious and committed, that can mean only trouble for the police in Soweto. But trouble's something Soweto knows something about.

"Soweto, Soweto, Soweto . . ." Running from police, scraping for food, aspiring, living, dying, crying—even residents lose their way in the song's lyrics.

In December 1976, Soweto students addressed a leaflet to "all fathers, mothers, brothers and sisters . . . in all cities, towns and villages in . . . South Africa":

We appeal to you to align yourself with the struggle for your own liberation. Be involved and be united with us, as it is your own son or daughter that we bury every weekend. Death has become a common thing to us all in the townships. There is no peace, there shall be none until we are free. . . .

OUR CALL IS ALL THINGS THAT WE ENJOY MUST BE SUSPENDED FOR THE SAKE OF OUR KIDS WHO DIED FROM POLICE BULLETS

—NO CHRISTMAS SHOPPING
—NO CHRISTMAS CARDS
—NO CHRISTMAS PRESENTS
—NO CHRISTMAS PARTIES
—NO SHEBEEN DRINKING

Let us, your kids, for the first time, neither buy nor put on any new clothing for Christmas or New Year.

This year 1976 shall go down into our history as the YEAR OF MOURN-ING, the year that flowed with sweat, blood and tears for our liberation.

That Christmas Thenjie was in detention in King William's Town, soon to be released and banned to her mother's home in Soweto.

"Soweto, Soweto" . . . years since Hector Peterson was shot. The people have not forgotten the children who led their parents. There is pride. They have not forgotten the children bleeding in the streets. There is bitterness.

Soweto is a symbol. A state of mind. A real place. Thenjie's home. Whites believe they control it.

Kitty Duma

10

The Wrong Comb

**The Afrikaners think they are liberal if they just say hello
to a black.** —*Kitty Duma, 1978*

K itty Duma is fond of using two succinct adjectives
to describe people—cold and warm. Cold applies
to some of her relatives and most whites. Warm is
for her mother, long since dead, for her minister's wife, who runs an
orphanage in Soweto, and for Hannah and Thenjie Mtintso.

Kitty must be like her mother. She is warm, friendly, and very
astute. She met Thenjie and her mother through my asking her to
deliver a set of earrings to Thenjie while she was in the Fort prison.

Unlike Thenjie, Kitty has known whites all her life because of
her mother's community work and probably because she has never
been as poor as Thenjie. She forms precise, and I think accurate,
judgments about whites, both when she meets them individually
and when she assesses them politically.

Kitty is six years older than apartheid, born in 1942, and she has
developed her political stance gradually. There is little in Thenjie's
philosophy that Kitty would dispute, but, unlike Thenjie, she does
not seek to confront the system. Rather, the system has forced her
into a canny resistance.

The political trial of her journalist husband Enoch Duma in
1978 tested Kitty's mettle and ripened her politics. Police snatched
him from bed in front of their children early one morning in 1977
and detained him without charge. After being tortured and spending
nine months in prison, he was finally tried and acquitted of charges
under the Terrorism Act.

I sat with Kitty through parts of his trial and marveled at her
sagacious courage and wit during the ordeal.

Kitty could tell Freda Van Rooyen a thing or two for her Kontak
organization. In fact, it was Kitty who charged that the Afrikaners are
not Christians, a charge that impelled Freda to have me discuss the

matter with her minister. "I disagree with this woman. I would like to meet her," Freda had said.

But Kitty would have none of it. She knew Freda's type. Unlike Thenjie, Kitty has worked with many whites, including Afrikaners. And she is a devout Anglican, perfectly capable of quoting the Bible back to any other Christian.

Kitty sat in my house and talked, waving a half-eaten chicken leg—chicken bought from "Kentucky Fried Chicken" until she read the *Post* newspaper story by journalist Zwelakhe Sisulu. The black people working for Kentucky Fried Chicken finished after 11 P.M.— past their curfew and too late to travel home to Soweto. Every night they were locked inside without toilet facilities or beds.

"What can whites do?" Kitty asked. "Why don't they rebel against this nonsense? Why do they always say there's nothing they can do?

"Because their life is too good. Ya, exactly. That's exactly it and not that they can't see or they can't hear. But they always say there's nothing they can do.

"There's nothing they can do!

"Maybe they are afraid to lose their superiority . . . afraid because they know black people are equal to them. They do know that. That's why they are afraid."

Kitty's eyes rivet the observer. Large, soft brown pupils ringed by pale blue irises. Her mother's eyes were like that, so were her uncle's, but no one else's of her African ancestors.

She sees things most whites do not and notices each discrimination as if it were new.

"I don't care if I never see her again," she said of one American who "kept using the word *nonwhite* for blacks."

Kitty was born on a black location in Roodeport, five miles from where she now lives in Dobsonville, Soweto. Her husband was born near Durban, in Natal.

The house in Roodeport was torn down in 1961 to make way for a white suburb. The government moved blacks out. At the time, Kitty was dating Enoch. Her mother, seeing they were likely to marry, placed Enoch's name on the permit for the government-designated house in Soweto. This was illegal. Enoch had not lived in Johannesburg long enough to qualify for a house.

A few years later, when Enoch had to be registered for a job, "the officials didn't understand why his name was on the house permit; he hadn't been in Soweto long enough. But nobody would question the superintendent who had okayed the forms."

Life is so bureaucratically complicated for a black that even people with legal training find it difficult to understand the much-amended pass laws with their obscure provisions and tortuous language.

"Would you change anything if you could repeat your life?" I asked.

"I would change my life completely. I wouldn't get married so young, at eighteen. I would struggle along even if I didn't have a father. I would try to carry on with my education."

In Kitty's parents' generation, the father made the decisions; the wife could say only yes. The wife had to call the husband "Father" like the children, and take whatever came from him. These were the old customs.

Today educated black women complain little about their lot as women because color is a more insistent issue. Kitty is aware of having fewer rights than the black man, but she knows she is better off than most black women.

She works four days a week for 220 rands ($253) a month at the office of the Campus Crusades for Christ. She speaks seven languages: English, Afrikaans, Xhosa, Zulu, Tswana, Sotho, and Pede. Campus Crusades, a California-based evangelist organization, provided teaching materials for South Africa's Dutch Reformed churches, including Gabrielle Malan's, as well as other Protestant congregations.

"What irritates me most is I find myself in an office with a white person who knows nothing but earns more than I do. I hate that. I do translations and secretarial work for the black lay ministries. I actually do a lot," Kitty said.

"We know Afrikaners inside out, but not intimately. You cannot have a relationship with an Afrikaner because of this *baaskap* or master kind of thing. An Afrikaner farmer may get to liking a laborer, but if they have a drink in his lounge, he will pour the black worker's drink into a mug. That's the kind of love they have. The Afrikaners think they are liberal if they just say hello to a black.

"I'd like to go into an Afrikaner's head and see how he looks at things," she said. "They don't see blacks as human beings. They don't. I always said if they had their way, they would just cut off black hands and let the hands work for them and do away with the blacks. But they can't do that."

"What about the Afrikaners you work with at Campus Crusades?"

"They are friendly at work. If you meet them outside they are different. At work, they just wear a mask. Like yesterday, I went to lunch and saw one girl who used to work there, an Afrikaner, a real

National Party supporter, you know. She left to get married; she said she would invite us to her house. I was wondering if she would. In fact, I said, 'Hi, Doreen' purposely and she didn't know what to do . . . it's their upbringing.

"The Christians are the worst in this country. This Campus Crusades—they came to South Africa and they work within the framework of the government, not the Bible."

"Is a person a Christian if he wants to kill Hitler? Or is a black a Christian if he wants to kill an Afrikaner?" I asked.

"You could not be a Christian if you wanted to kill," Kitty said. "Look, Jesus didn't say things directly. Everything was in parables."

"Would Jesus have accepted apartheid?"

"No, if he had, he would have come as a king. He was in a position to own thousands of slaves, but he didn't. Why did he choose to be a servant and die for the sinners? He said, 'Your ways are not my ways.'

"You learn not to go along with what the white man does with the Bible. You must go according to what the Bible tells you. Mind you, not only white people use the Bible for their own ends; our own black people do too. Those independent African churches with their mammoth memberships are mostly headed by illiterates. If you can swindle, people will follow you."

She was referring to a few of the hundreds of free-lance churches that pepper the Soweto landscape. Every weekend thousands of Africans don white flowing uniforms with colored sashes and shoulder loops. They parade through the streets of Soweto singing, chanting, dancing to drums. They march through Johannesburg, where whites toss coins to the celebrants from their apartment windows.

As a child Kitty was a Methodist. When she moved to Kimberley she switched to the Anglican Church. "Why?" I asked.

"I think Anglicans are concerned with better things than competing with other Christians for minor things. They are more involved with the people."

"Do you think God is on the side of the black man?" I asked.

"He is!"

"Is God on the side of the white man?"

"He's not. When you sit and think—I'm not judging—but surely God is on our side because we're not doing the bad things. At this stage, I could be against religion because of what I've seen. But religion is one thing you cannot control in a human being. If a person believes, you cannot take it away from him easily."

"Aren't you trained to your beliefs?" I asked.

Kitty described her friend, who refused to accept the opinions of others without reasoning for herself and who, by example, taught her to do the same.

"But opinions are different than beliefs. You see, years ago, before the white man came here, the black people believed in God in their own way. But the missionaries surely confused everybody—which is why you find people believing in ancestors and in God at the same time. There was someone called Qamatha in Xhosa, which was, I would say, God, a supreme being."

"Why don't you go back and accept that religion?"

"How can I go back to Qamatha? I don't know what they did about Qamatha. The only history books written then were by white people. Poor black people had only storytellers, old men; I think it's lost. If you were a historian, maybe you could find it in the mountains. Unfortunately, with African people, we're not as adventurous as white people."

"After a revolution, will Christianity endure in South Africa? Or do you think the country will become Marxist?"

"I don't want to answer that one. We don't know. These young people don't feel they have to go to church. It's a phase. Once they get older what are they going to do?

"Take my niece Diane: a girl died at her university. Most of the students there were Marxists. But when they went to pray for that girl the hall was full. Why? These people were not supposed to believe in God—so why were they there?

"It's a hard road we're walking, very hard. How can they possibly be Christians and do the things they do? How can they believe in Jesus when they discriminate the way they do?

"When I was young, my brother was killed by a man who lived in the same township. When I saw him . . . it registered . . . but I didn't hate him. My parents were not ones to organize against him. You see, in South Africa if you kill another black, it doesn't matter; only when you kill a white, you have to hang.

"Apartheid affects everything . . . everything, everything. You've always got to restrain yourself. If I want to go to Cape Town with you, I have to think . . . the police there . . . are they active or what? Just the whole thing. I'm not worried about parks or cinemas. It's this undermining of one's brain because of the color of your skin. That is what bugs me, because you find it all over.

"Go to black and white policemen. You'll find the black is doing more work. The white is too stupid to know what's happening. Go to a road worker. The white is standing counting stars or having coffee and he earns twenty times more than the black. Look at every situation. It is frustrating."

Kitty and Enoch Duma and others like them have been described by advertising and promotion agencies as "up market" blacks—that is, urban blacks who aspire to better education, travel, and consumer goods. The Dumas have a house, a car, a television, a stereo, and a telephone. They also have a servant, to enable Kitty to work outside the home. Yet, behind the advertising label is a desire by the government to make "up market" urban blacks into a middle-class buffer—a separate faction with a self-interest in acquiescing to apartheid. The theory, postulated by many liberals and some Afrikaners, does not reflect the black reality.

To Kitty, "black people, whatever their work, face the same problem, white racism.

"Actually, we've been brought up with this thing that dark is awful. I think it came from the missionaries. They did a lot of harm in this place. They did a lot of harm. They associated light to white. I've always thought, who said these were black people? Who said these were white people?

"Just take the use of a comb. For years we had been using the wrong comb—one that came from the missionaries. Before going to school, you suffered under this comb. If you went without combing your hair, the teacher would grab a comb and go through your hair mercilessly.

"Rural people still use a mielie cob. When they've eaten all the mielies, the cob is dried. Usually they keep their hair very short and the cob is like a brush. The Shangaans are the ones who started making this comb, which is like an Afro comb.

"If you've noticed, a lot of people don't wear wigs these days. The one with long hair used to be the 'in' thing. But now you feel uncomfortable wearing them.

"The first people to wear wigs were trying to be colored. If you were a colored you could get employed. You could get better money.

"I'll tell you about Coronation Hospital. It used to be an all-black hospital until they moved blacks from Johannesburg to Soweto; then it became a colored hospital. At that time they didn't have colored nurses because coloreds earned more at the factories. So the black nurses with lighter skin were kept on. They were taken by the matron to Pretoria and given colored identities to work in Coronation Hospital."

I asked Kitty what she thought about the Black Consciousness Movement.

She said she began to relate to it when she saw how it affected the image blacks had of themselves. "They were no longer being brainwashed.

"But at first I didn't like Black Consciousness because they were very extreme. Then I went to the National Black Theater Conference in Durban. Strini Moodley and Saths Cooper, who are now imprisoned on Robben Island, were there. They are great actors. Ya, they did a lot of Malcolm X plays and they are very good. Enoch went as a reporter. I was working for Phoenix Players (a theater group). At this conference they were totally antiwhite. They were saying we don't want anything to do with white people.

"A friend, talking to one of the leaders, an Indian, said, 'Gee, what a nice car you have. Where did you get it?' He said, 'Grosvenor Motors.' My friend pointed out that was a white company. Why didn't the man get his car at Mr. Naidoo's instead of from a white?

"To be frank, what I knew about Black Consciousness I had read in the papers or got from Enoch. That was my first time with the people. And I wasn't aware till then that it included Indians as well.

"I felt it should be completely black if it did want to be black. To start with, Indians have better opportunities than we have. I couldn't understand how Indians could be as involved as black people. But I think Indians are better than coloreds about being involved.

"You see the problem with coloreds is they want to be white. But the whites won't accept them. Because of that you can't trust coloreds. If it came to a choice, they would choose to help the white man. They would never choose to help the black man. They don't want to acknowledge there is black blood in them.

"I've known coloreds all my life. I went to school in Kimberley. It was the Cape, there were a lot of coloreds there. Everybody spoke Afrikaans and went to school in English.

"I'll tell you what they do . . . the coloreds are not . . . I'm sorry, maybe I'm sounding terrible, but this is what I feel about them. They aren't honest people. For instance, a colored whom we know comes out to a township. He says he's black. But you go to where he lives and he doesn't even want to know you because you are black. Maybe there are exceptions.

"The Afrikaners feel closer to coloreds because they speak Afrikaans. In Cape Town they use the same facilities as whites. I've heard coloreds can use white buses, but not blacks. I don't know, I've never been to Cape Town. This is just a sick society. You find someone blacker than I am, but because he speaks Afrikaans he is colored.

"I don't blame the young guys who say, 'Away with whites.' They never had contact with whites to know they are people—some of them—or so we thought.

"But all whites are part of the oppressor camp, really, in South Africa, especially liberals. They are worst.

"When I was little I always asked my mother, 'Why do the

Nationalists win?' It means these liberal English are voting them in. I was young then. Every time an election came, my parents would be so enthusiastic, hoping the opposition would win over the Nationalists. But these people, the English, were not honest. They were the ones who were voting for the Nationalists. Nobody seemed to see it then.

"Actually, I hate people who have double standards or who won't talk the truth. I feel politicians are liars."

I pointed out that she was being pulled more and more into politics because of Enoch's job as a journalist and his trial.

"Being black you find you just have to be in politics," Kitty admitted.

One November night when air and body temperatures were not at odds, and the full moon rolled over Johannesburg as if the east-to-west streets were set up as a guide, Kitty lost her pass book.

Her "dompas," the identity assigned her by Afrikaner Nationalists, had been in her rust-orange corduroy handbag, which had disappeared.

"Do you realize what a hassle it is to get these documents duplicated?" Kitty asked in despair. She had just taken off three days from work to obtain the documents needed to travel to the neighboring black-ruled country of Lesotho.

Her pass book, which she must carry at all times, lists her as a Xhosa, born in 1942, classification number 10 (1) (a). However, applying for the travel documents, she was asked to produce her marriage certificate. The Afrikaner bureaucrat discovered she was married to a Zulu and promptly transformed her into a Zulu on her travel papers.

A Xhosa for thirty-six years, she became a Zulu overnight, a true apartheid chrysalis into a butterfly. It made her giggle.

But losing her documents was no joke. "We've got to pray," she said, deciding to search in the last places we had been.

There was no purse at the Value Supermarket or in the Fontana Inn Food Shop. We trudged glumly downhill through a stream of pedestrians. Some were black prostitutes from nearby massage parlors; others, guests from the Johannesburger Hotel, which hosted Japanese and German tours. The Japanese were classified "honorary whites" by the government while visiting South Africa.

Suddenly Kitty remembered the hotel lobby pay phone and dashed back. A black doorman in a top hat guided her to the reception desk. They handed over the purse. A small amount of money was missing. Kitty was too relieved about finding the documents to care about the money. But something extra was in her handbag. She lifted it out, then dropped it into my palm. It was the skeleton key to the white toilet in the hotel. On it was marked "European females." Obviously, a white woman had stolen Kitty's money, gone to the toilet, and inadvertently dropped the bathroom key into the wrong purse, Kitty's purse.

Kitty looked at the key with disgust.

Tiny Mchunu

Roslyn Mabiletsa

Eunice Mazibuko

11

They Want

to Be Called

"Madam"

You always know: I'm an unwanted person in this house. They just want my strength. *—Eunice Mazibuko, 1979*

T henjie never, in all our conversations, discussed domestic servants. She had never had any, and any she knew were neighbors.

Kitty told me she once had a servant who stole and she had to fire her. One day when I entered Kitty's house in Soweto and had failed to greet her servant, the woman retreated to another room and cried. Kitty explained that my failure to say hello was considered the height of rudeness. But otherwise Kitty did not mention her servants although she had had several over the years, who lived in her small house, cleaning it and tending to the children while Kitty worked at jobs in Johannesburg.

In contrast, white women talk endlessly about their "girls"—at lunch, bridge, tea, church meetings, the swimming pool. Stories about stealing, witchraft, pregnancies, illegitimate children, the occasional murder. The white women thrive on the repetitive gossip. Usually the only blacks that whites know are their servants, and it is from them that whites form almost all their opinions of black South African society.

There is a terrible joke whites tell about servants: A white woman coaxingly asks, "Maria, you like madam, don't you? You wouldn't kill madam if there were a revolution, would you?" To which Maria sweetly replies, "Oh no, madam. I could never kill you. I would kill the madam next door, and her girl would kill you."

"The majority of black women (several million) are employed in domestic service or on farms, but employment statistics never include them," Roberta Johnson said. She was co-convener of the Women's Legal Status Committee.

"Domestics have no standards of employment, no minimum wage, no membership in the unemployment fund, and no umbrella organizations. They simply are not counted."

A few years ago a survey found education for most domestic servants never went beyond standard two. "Now if you haven't gone beyond standard two," Roberta said, "you are almost illiterate because what you have learned you forget."

She concluded that if a minimum wage were insisted upon, it would "price the domestic servant clean out of the market, the way it did in every country in the world. As it is, a domestic has housing, food, clothing, soap, hot water—the basic things."

Roberta Johnson believes the majority of the servants couldn't possibly keep their children with them. "How many of us (whites) are prepared to have six, seven children living in? It would be very nice if they could live down the road in their own little flat. But they can't. This is where apartheid comes in. They've got to live in Soweto."

The families of female domestics live without the mother, either with a relative in a homeland, as Thenjie did when her mother sent her to the Transkei, or with someone in a township.

There are white women, mostly liberals, who are concerned about the plight of servants. In 1973 the Domestic Workers' Employment Project (DWEP), connected with the Institute of Race Relations, set up Centers of Concern in churches, synagogues, and halls in the large cities of South Africa. In Johannesburg about ten thousand domestic workers belong to DWEP. The group's growth alarmed conservative whites. At the centers, white women from northern suburbs teach black servants housekeeping etiquette: flower arranging, pattern cutting, and the like—and elementary reading as well.

Inevitably when these black women domestics meet at the centers, they compare working conditions and salaries. In 1978, a DWEP announcement stated servants should receive a minimum monthly wage of 65 rands ($75). This irritated many whites, and DWEP organizers received obscene phone calls and threats against their lives. The authorities have warned several times that they might shut down the centers. However, the churches have stood firm, so far, and the government has backed off.

The late Dr. Ellen Hellman, once executive director of the liberal Institute of Race Relations, noted that organizations such as DWEP are not going to change the political structure in South Africa. "But it's a worthwhile input."

However, she described DWEP as "a completely one-sided organization. It deals only with the rights of domestic workers and hardly touches the question of workers' obligations. It doesn't deal with the many problems that arise: the quarreling between servants on tribal or other grounds; the witchcraft accusations . . . all sorts of family relations."

Preston White of Durban carried out studies on domestic workers that revealed a suburban hierarchy. "Some servants won't work anywhere but the northern suburbs—"the so-called mink and manure belt," Dr. Hellman said.

"Do you realize to what extent loneliness is mitigated in this country? Go to a shopping center and see the number of old women—you know we live longer than men. The women are arthritic and so forth; they hobble around; or they are wheeled around by black helpers, cooks, maids. You can see how friendly they are. These old women have someone. They give driving lessons to their black helpers. A real friendship develops. If you were to analyze it, friendship really is a need for each other in some way. Well, isn't that at the very heart of many relationships?"

A young white woman summarized a common attitude of whites, especially poor whites, toward their servants:

"You know, right up there near Brixton there are tiny houses, funny, little pokey places. People who live there obviously haven't got too much to come and go on, but believe me, they have their domestic servants. There's always a black lady sweeping out the front. It's part of the whole status thing. As long as you are a white madam, that's social status enough. Who needs to go into competition with men? You know you are better than all those black women. So?"

So, what about that terrible joke? Will blacks rise up and kill their madams? Can Thenjie, who advocates nonviolence, find support from the less literate of her people? Or if she found sympathy, would it be negated by fear?

Through assistance from organizers at DWEP, I located three domestic servants from the white suburbs of Johannesburg.

Tiny Mchunu, age forty-one, is a domestic worker at the Wayburn house. Eunice Mazibuko, thirty-six, works for Alicia Gordon. Roslyn Mabiletsa, thirty-four, works for the Leebs family. The three women met in my apartment for the interview in early 1979. They did not belong to DWEP but had formed their own small domestic servants' club called Inthuthuko (Progressive).

Tiny, president of the club, noted membership had dropped drastically. She speculated that the members would rather spend their one full day off per week in other ways.

Traditional *doeks* (scarves) covered their heads. They wore nylons, medium-heeled shoes, dressy dresses. We gathered around the tape recorder.

If she had a choice, Tiny would rather drive a taxi; Eunice would live with her children in the countryside; and Roslyn seemed content with her life.

Eunice likes her madam's dogs, chows with navy-blue tongues. "They don't bite," she insisted to Tiny, who, like most Africans, detests dogs because they are often trained to attack Africans.

Eunice grew up in Danhauser, Natal, with her grandmother. At twelve she joined her parents in Soweto. She became a domestic servant in 1965 at age twenty-three, for 18 rands ($20.75) a month. Today she receives 65 rands ($74.75) a month and lives in a room she considers too small at the Gordon house.

Tiny earns 70 rands ($80.50) a month and lives in. She has worked twenty-seven years for the same Jewish family, helping to rear the Wayburns' son. Tiny knows the white family votes "Nat" (National Party). She is asking for higher wages, but is running into opposition.

"Mrs. Wayburn said to me, 'Oh, it's just because you've got a car; that's why you feel your money is not enough.' I say to her, 'You're talking nonsense. We don't talk about my car. My car is my car. I'm talking about the money, about pay for the job; don't talk about my car. You don't know where I got money to buy that car. Now, you got nothing to do with that car.'"

Tiny would like to leave the Wayburns.

"What would you do?" I asked.

"I'd do my own job. Selling; driving. I'd go back to Natal to my house and do sewing and bake cakes and sell it to the school. If I got enough money, I'd change my car and get a big one like a taxi. I told the Wayburns if I left them, I don't want to work for another woman."

Eunice has been a servant to British, German, and Jewish families. She found her present job with Alicia Gordon in early 1978.

Roslyn lived in Sophiatown until she was ten, when the location was razed to make way for a white suburb. She attended school on a farm near Brits, north of Pretoria. In 1966, at age twenty-two, she returned to Johannesburg to work. In Rosebank her first salary was 16 rands ($18.40) a month. In 1968, she moved to the Leeb family in Rouxville. They hired her at 25 rands a month. "They give me a raise every month. Now I'm getting 130 rands ($150) a month." There are seven people in the Leeb family, including a ninety-one-year-old grandfather from Zambia.

According to the Chamber of Commerce 1978 calculations, in Soweto the minimum wage needed for a family of six to live was 174 rands ($200) a month. The Institute for Planning Research estimated that the same family of six would need 271.71 rands ($260) in 1982.

On her $74.75, Eunice supports her mother, a sick father, and two sons in Soweto.

Roslyn supports her parents and two children who live on a farm in Brits.

Tiny maintains her second daughter, who attends Marianhill school in Natal—one of the best schools for Africans. The fees are 200 rands per year, nearly one-fourth of Tiny's total income.

Of the three women, only Eunice is married. Her husband earns 45 rands ($51.75) per week and lives with her at the Gordon home, although the children do not.

"They can be with me on school holidays," Eunice said. "It's against the law other times. Even your husband is not allowed to stay with you in the rooms. But Mrs. Gordon allows it. Most of them allow men to stay, the husband or the boyfriend, but it's against the law."

"Have the police bothered you?" I asked.

"The police did come while I was with my husband," Eunice remembered. "They say I must pay 14 rands because I'm the one who told my husband to come and sleep with me. And he must pay 14 rands. I paid 14 because I'm the one who told my husband . . ." All the women laughed.

"Would you like to be with your children?" I asked Eunice.

"I'd be very happy to stay with my family, but not in Soweto. I prefer the country, the farm. I like being outside where it's nice and quiet; I'm just here in town for money."

In South Africa, every other Sunday and each Thursday are traditionally maids' days off. But on their Sundays off servants must first make the beds. Tiny said on her free Sundays she is not free before 10 A.M..

"They don't know how to make beds because they never have since they were born," Eunice said. "If they make the bed you can laugh."

"They can't even pick up their clothes," Tiny added. "They just take them off and leave them. We must pick up everything and tidy up."

The women agreed that neither the Jewish nor the English "madams" like the servants to keep babies with them.

"The Afrikaners don't mind as much," Roslyn said. "But you know why they don't care? It's because they don't pay you. Afrikaners say you can stay with your friend, can do what you like, but when you complain about money, they say you eat here, wash here, sleep here, everything. They're clever that way."

"Do the women you work for cook?" I asked.

"Some of them cook," Tiny said. "If they cook, they put a book on the stove and read it before they put salt in the pot. But they don't wash. They take this glass, they put it in the sink; they take another one, drink out of it; they take another one, they drink."

"They can't rinse," Eunice elaborated.

"You must follow them like babies," Tiny said.

"And when you do the same thing and she comes into the kitchen and finds three or four glasses dirty, she doesn't like that. If it's you, it's wrong. If it's her, it's right," Eunice said.

"The English people know how to work," Eunice said. "They help a lot."

"They carry the trays so you can wash up quickly and go have a rest," Roslyn agreed.

"The thing I like about the German and English people—when your friend comes to visit, she'll invite you to come inside and sit and talk to you; sometimes she will make you a cup of tea. But the Jewish people are not that way," Roslyn said.

"Have any of you felt close to the families you have worked for?" I asked.

Tiny: "Yes, I'm very close with them."

Eunice: "The trouble is this apartheid. Even if you're close, you just think to yourself, oh, I'm black, that's white. It's apartheid. Even if you're close to her, you think about yourself and she's white. Even if you are big friends there's something in the middle."

Tiny: "You can't be friends. You can't eat with them; you can't touch their food. You can't touch their dishes. You must have your own dishes. Separate. They must have their own things."

Eunice: "And that shows you that you are black. You always know: I'm an unwanted person in this house. They just want my strength."

Tiny: "You can't use their towels. You can't eat their food. They buy your meat. They call it chuckers meat. Our own meat. It is cheaper. They get it special for us."

"What does it taste like?" I asked.

Roslyn: "It takes a long time to cook. And you cut and cut and cut that meat."

Tiny: "You go to the butcher and get their meat and servants' meat. They call it servants' meat. They write 'servants' on the label. You don't know whether you eat good meat or old or bad."

Eunice: "It's horse meat."

Roslyn: "Sometimes it smells funny. You think maybe it is horse meat or something."

Tiny: "You just eat it like you eat chewing gum."

Roslyn: (laughing) "Unsweetened chewing gum."

Eunice: "But I did complain to my madam. She asked me, 'How is the meat, Eunice?' I said, 'I don't like the meat.' She said, 'Okay, what kind of meat do you like?' I said I would like brisket. Brisket is very nice. It's fatty, but it's nicer. Then she changed the meat to brisket. But if she forgets to tell the butcher, they send servants' meat and you must complain again."

Roslyn: "When she comes with the meat I tell her I don't want this. She says, 'The butcher said black people always like this meat.' I said, 'I don't like it.'"

"What else do they feed you, any vegetables?" I asked.

Tiny: "They buy mielie meal for us. They know we like mielie meal, mielie pap, and meat. Sometimes, they say you can take one potato or two potatoes; otherwise, they say mielies. You can't touch vegetables. You just cook your meat, that's all."

Eunice: "If they are not kosher, you can cook in the house. But if they are kosher, they don't want your meat in their kitchen because their meat is koshered and yours is not."

The three women made certain their children attended Sunday school every week.

Roslyn: "When I'm working, my parents go to church every Sunday and they take the children with them."

Tiny: (laughing) "They must do what I do; if I go to a witch, they must do the same thing."

The women giggled.

I asked if they indeed did go to sangomas (practitioners of witchcraft).

Eunice: "Of course we do. There is sickness which sometimes keeps going and going. But you don't get better until you take your own thing. You were born like that. We know our witch doctors; we don't know the white doctors. We try the doctors first . . . maybe both. We use them both because, surely, there's sickness the doctor can't cure."

Tiny, who has a boyfriend, said, "I don't want to get married. It's useless. A man wants seven wives. Today he's this side, tomorrow he's that. What are you going to do with him? Oh, I don't like it. I don't want to marry. I'll just get somebody to come and go. See, it's wasting time to get married. In Soweto lots of men run away. They leave their wives and kids."

Eunice has been married ten years. "She's lucky," Roslyn said.

But all has not been smooth. "You know, when somebody does something wrong, you just keep quiet," Eunice said, explaining how she had kept her husband so long. "My husband used to run around with not one girlfriend but girlfriends. Maybe he thought I would find a boyfriend somewhere. But he always found me alone; I just kept quiet until he changed."

"I couldn't stand it," Tiny said of the girlfriends.

"People are not the same," Eunice said. "I'm not blaming Tiny. I keep quiet; now he's very good, you won't believe it. The people who knew him those years will not believe that's Solomon. It's not easy, but I tried it."

"What do you call the white women you work for?" I asked.

"They want to be called 'madam,' " Roslyn said.

"I was once working for Mrs. Lancaster; I never said madam to her; I never said master to him," Eunice recalled. "I just called them Jimmy and Lydia. She didn't like you to call her madam. It was the first and last time. It's nice really; you don't feel like a servant. You feel at home. We had the same age children. Their child was Henry; they got two high chairs, one for my child, my baby. When we ate, we sat at the table and put the high chairs next to us to feed our babies. They were foreigners, from England," Eunice said. "I think the Afrikaners show the world they're Christians, but their hearts are not Christian. They are very hard to us. They are standing on us."

Then she added, "Anyway, things are getting better than it was. Like the parks, maybe you've seen them. Things are a little bit better than before, but most of the things are still the same.

Tiny: "They don't want our children to go to the same schools."

Eunice: "That's right, or live in the same places."

"If there were no more apartheid, who would you want to head the government?" I asked.

"Black or white, as long as he's doing the right thing," Eunice said. "Even if he's white you don't mind as long as he's doing what is good for everyone, not what is good for them. The rule must be for everyone, not the good rules for whites and the bad rules for blacks."

"Do you know about Rhodesia, what is happening there?" I asked.

"We know they're fighting for the terrorists to come to jump the border," Eunice said. "Maybe—I don't know if I'm right or wrong—the Russians want to come into South Africa to have South Africa be under them. And I don't think in Rhodesia they are trying to stop that. That's what I heard on Bantu radio."

"I think they are just fighting for their own rights," Tiny said. "Like freedom, that's all."

"Are you on the side of the guerrillas?" I asked.

"Me?" Tiny said. "I'm just in the middle."

"It's not easy to understand," Eunice said, "because the blacks kill each other."

"They don't want the whites in Rhodesia," Tiny said. "They will go, of course," she added.

"Do you think whites will leave South Africa?" I asked.

"Then who's going to help us?" Tiny said.

"I don't think so; I don't think they must leave," Eunice said.

"We must live together because if we live without them, we will just be fighting," Roslyn said. "All the chiefs will come together and fight. It's better when the whites stay."

"How are South African blacks going to win their freedom?" I asked.

"We have to fight for it," Eunice said, very softly.

"The thing is this, we want freedom," Roslyn said. "Some don't understand what freedom is. If everybody can know what freedom is, it would be easy for black people. But most don't understand. Two years back in Soweto, some of them knew what they were fighting for; some didn't know."

"You can't read the truth in the newspapers," Tiny said.

"On the radio," Eunice said, "when a hundred people are dead, the news tells you fifty. They never tell you the truth. But when you listen to the news from Botswana then they tell you everything about Johannesburg, what's going on.

"The Post doesn't tell the truth. I think it's because the black reporters just write what the white says because they can't write the truth. If they write the truth they get into trouble. Like Qoboza—he used to tell the truth, he ends up in jail."

"Have you heard of Steve Biko?" I asked.

"Yes, I know of him a little bit," Eunice said. "I used to read about him in Drum magazine. I know he was a member of—what is it? BPC [Black People's Convention]. I don't know why they put him in jail. Well, I know a little bit, that they killed him because he was clever. They don't like a clever person because they open each and everyone's eyes. Nelson Mandela was clever. So I think he was also the same thing. He's not one of my leaders, but I respect him," Eunice said. "Mandela was Xhosa," she added.

"He can't be your leader?" I said.

"He can. He can because he's black. He fights for South Africa, not for himself," Eunice said.

"He stands for everybody," Tiny said.

"We don't know about the others. We know about our leaders. We are Zulus, we know that our leader is clever," Eunice said. "Chief Buthelezi, they nearly took him to jail because he is clever."

"We're not allowed to talk about Nelson Mandela," Eunice concluded.

"Why?" I asked.

"You know too much if you talk about him," Tiny said.

"I mean to say, it's not very good to talk about him," Eunice said. "If you do, it means you know something. They'll take you to tell them more. So we must be careful. You must turn stupid."

The family Thenjie left behind in Soweto every time she was detained—her
mother Hannah Mtintso, her cousin Thamie Coha, and her son Lumumba

12

Afrikaners,

Liberals, and

Going to Jail

People say, "Use multiracialism as a means." I say it can't
be a means because it is the end. It is what we are trying to
establish.   —*Thenjie Mtintso, 1979*

T henjie has talked substantively with only three
Afrikaners in her life. But the first two encounters
were not as "strenuous" as her meeting with Ry-
kie Van Reenen, an assistant editor for the Afrikaans newspaper
Rapport.

Miss Van Reenen writes what Afrikaners consider to be *verligte,*
eloquent, and elegant newspaper columns. She met Steve Biko before he was killed and, Thenjie said, "She thought he was the most
intelligent guy she has ever talked to in the black or white community."

Thenjie described her as elderly and charming, but she "was on
guard against being angry with her for being naïve—for her being in
this country for so long and perhaps pretending not to know the
problems.

"Another strain came from having to explain the obvious to her.
When that happens, you know the person is playing with words,
going in circles. It is the same with American politicians who come
here. They know exactly what is happening here and what they
ought to do, but they always hide and evade our call for them to
remove their investments that are propping up apartheid."

Thenjie said she thought Miss Van Reenen could return to her community and "tell the Broeders" that her views on a sharing of the land and her antagonism toward the system were representative of a high percentage of blacks.

Although she assured Miss Van Reenen she would be glad to talk with her again any time, she poured cold water over the Afrikaner's suggestion of contacts between blacks and whites on a professional basis, e.g., teachers, journalists.

"White teachers and black have nothing in common with one another," Thenjie argued. "The first priority for us is our blackness. We have to solve the black problem before we solve the teachers' problem.

"Just because we are women doesn't mean we have anything in common. Your child and my child are poles apart. I worry because my son may become a tsotsi (hoodlum). My child is being influenced by the environment in Soweto. Do you have those problems? You don't. So what are we going to talk about? Recipes? A la king? I don't have enough money to make à la king. I'm going home tonight and cook pap and vleis (corn meal and meat). Your maid is going to be cooking for you, so what are we going to talk about? Nothing."

Thenjie explained to me her inflexibility toward Miss Van Reenen:

"There was a time in this country when whites had the upper hand. Now we do. They come to us. We say we are not ready to meet you. Now they fear us. We did not fear them, but we hated them. Now we hate them no more. We don't care about them. We are on our own. It is a time in this country when whites wish to be black."

I suspect Thenjie was not as harsh in her manner as she was in her political position, if only because she said Miss Van Reenen was older than she expected. Like most Africans, Thenjie displays respect for age, even if she thinks the older person is not admirable.

But the door was virtually shut to one of the most *verligte* women in the Afrikaner community, even as Kitty had vigorously shaken her head no when told that Freda would like to meet her.

Another white woman who tried to meet Thenjie was Helen Suzman, the woman who personifies liberalism in South Africa. As a member of Parliament for the Progressive (then the Progressive Federal) Party, Mrs. Suzman fought in defense of blacks' rights for more than a quarter of a century.

Thenjie was in the Fort prison in Johannesburg during November 1977, after being detained without charge on October 19, when prison wardens came to inform her that Helen Suzman wanted to visit the black women political prisoners.

In a flash Thenjie organized all the women with her to say no, all except for Ellen Khuzwayo, a social worker sometimes called the "mother of Soweto." Mrs. Khuzwayo was much older than the other detained women and, although a long-time vigorous opponent of apartheid, she was not a member of the Black Consciousness Movement. Thenjie said she reasoned with Mrs. Khuzwayo to join them, but the old woman still believed in communication with whites. A case of generation gap and ideology, for Mrs. Khuzwayo even allowed herself to be visited by the man who detained her without charge—the Minister of Police and Justice, Jimmy Kruger, a most detested man in Soweto, the man who signed Thenjie's banning orders.

"The very fact that Helen Suzman wanted to see us toward the end of November (the whites' general election was November 30) was funny," Thenjie said. "We'd been in the Fort all this time and I had been banned for ages. I think it was a political stance. It was not genuine."

Thenjie claims that liberals in the PFP actually favor apartheid but couch their version of segregation in subtler language.

"They agree to the concept of different groups of people. For instance, they don't want a unitary state, but think that we've got to be a confederation.

"Even if Helen and her gang came to power, they would give us concessions and lull the community into believing things have improved. We don't want concessions. We want a complete overhaul of the system. I'd rather have the Nats, and among the Nats, I'd rather have the *verkramptes*. That way the issues are clearer."

Thenjie said she had nothing against Helen Suzman personally but objected vehemently to her operating within the ambit of the PFP.

"I don't recognize liberals as people who are working for my liberation. They can never deliver me from the hand of the Nationalists. They are part and parcel of the system. In fact, they have delayed our liberation because for a long time the black man looked up to the Progs who devised partial solutions for our problems."

"People who are victimized for pass offenses will say to liberal white lawyers who defend them: 'Thank you, baas; oh, thank you, baas.'" Thenjie clapped her hands softly in the tribal method of thank you and bowed her head in mock subservience.

"Whatever we have to do in this country, be it on the economic, social, or political level, it has to be by blacks, for blacks, period.

"Black nationalists do not favor black/white mixing at this stage of the struggle. Whites must work within their own communities to change people's thinking. Whites don't need to have a banned black female talk about detention. People have been in jail in South Africa for years.

"The mistake of liberal whites has been to direct themselves to blacks. They have always seen the black 'problem'; they have not seen the white problem. The problem in this country is not a black problem. It is a white one."

"Can whites understand if they don't meet with blacks?" I asked.

"We have met before and it has not worked. It is always the same, with whitey up there and black down here. We come together and pretend. Look at Women for Peace, a multiracial organization, taking our children to visit Houghton (the rich white suburb which Helen Suzman represents in Parliament). The children adopt white standards. You never see a white child adopt black standards. They say they are trying to teach kids that color is not important, that you can mix freely. But the point of departure is the white standard.

"That type of multiracialism is not genuine. It's just assimilation of black into white. First we have to change. People say, 'Use multiracialism as a means.' I say, it can't be a means because it is the end. It is what we are trying to establish.

"We are going to take power in this country. It doesn't matter how long it takes us. During our struggle for freedom, we will learn who are our friends and who are our enemies."

Thenjie contends the West could shorten the struggle by withdrawing financial investments from South Africa.

"These investors prop up this government. They should dismiss the myth that blacks will suffer if they disinvest. We cannot suffer more than we do already. It's like a guy who is on the floor: he can't fall any further. Let's say blacks must continue suffering 50 percent for twenty years. We might as well suffer 70 percent for five years.

"In the Black People's Movement we are neither for the East nor for the West, but when it comes to the crux of the matter, we have to have help from somewhere. We have never expected America or Germany to help win our liberation. But we want them to know where we stand. We don't want to import liberation, but we can tell everybody what he can do in his own limited way. If he does not do it, it's no skin off our bodies."

Like other black nationalists Thenjie can suggest Western withdrawal of investments, but she doesn't expect that to happen to a great degree.

Before her detention in Potchefstroom, I had not asked Thenjie anything about what she had endured in her previous detentions, but I knew some of what other blacks had suffered.

Thenjie had been imprisoned five times without charge inside a two-year time span, once for four and a half months and once for ten months. She was allowed out hardly long enough to raise an *amandla* fist, let alone cause vast damage to apartheid.

And now she was in for the fifth time. She had written me a letter from Potchefstroom prison, saying she had asked the police to put me on the list of people to be allowed to visit her.

We drove through dull mining countryside south of Johannesburg: Thenjie's son Lumumba, her friend Rebecca (Reebs) Musi, and her cousin Thamie Coha, a nurse in the maternity ward at Baragwanath Hospital.

Thamie, in her forties and missing several teeth—which did not inhibit her bubbling laughter—told me nurses bring the highest *lobolla* or bride price in the black community because of their secure jobs. However, she said, her wage was not enough to support her mother, herself, and two children. Her husband was killed in 1974, when a car he was in collided with a truck.

"A white nurse earns 600 rands ($690) a month; a black nurse with ten years' experience gets 241 rands ($277). Rice, powdered milk—they cost the same whether you're white or black," Thamie said. "We think of that and start cursing everybody."

Approaching Potchefstroom, the two-lane road widened into a four-lane avenue with tall, shepherd-crook street lamps.

We parked on Kerk Street and headed over to the security police office behind Wimpy's restaurant.

Thamie, who had been there before, pressed the buzzer. A woman opened the door. Thamie requested permission for us to visit Thenjie. Thamie and Reebs handed over their pass books. The woman shut the door. We waited ten minutes. The woman returned with permits for Thamie and Lumumba. The police had refused Thenjie's written request that Reebs and I be allowed to visit.

We walked through the building in search of a toilet. A white woman leaving one, locked the door behind her. We asked to use it. She said no. Thamie asked a black woman. "The third floor has a toilet with no lock," she whispered, looking around nervously.

Wherever we walked, one white and two black women, white people stared at us with hostility.

Thamie wore a pumpkin-orange Xhosa dress. On her *doek*, a four-inch frill of black and orange beads dangled as a brooch. "When I wear this, Thenjie's friends say I'm being black conscious," she laughed.

Lumumba tagged along wearing the orange and black bead neck-lace Thamie had made for him the night before.

We went into Wimpy's. Four white men surrounded us until we left with our thick, pink guava juice in paper cups. Back in the street, Thamie burst out laughing. "Blacks must never enter the front door. We must order food from a side window." She pointed.

Then because Thamie wanted to buy wine, we entered a liquor shop. A woman behind the counter stared angrily at Thamie and Reebs, and said, "You go to the other side." We were in the *slegs blankes* (whites only) section. She turned to serve me.

"We are together," I said. The woman hesitated, scowled, then grudgingly asked Thamie, "What do you want?"

Thamie and Reebs were enjoying using my presence to snub the usual humiliations of petty apartheid.

We drove to a street without parking meters to eat our lunch. Lumumba was sleepy. He had visited his mother in prison many times and it was always a serious business for him.

We watched a black woman lumber down the street with a small white girl clutching her hand; on the woman's wide back, a white baby bobbed in a blanket.

"See that woman?" Thamie said. "They let her raise the chil-dren; then at a certain age they tell the children that blacks stink."

We drove three miles to the other end of Kerk Street, where the road led to the prison, a rectangular building of new, blond bricks lying low on the flat land. At the entrance, a black man watered dusty zinnias.

Inside we were directed to wait on a bench, with our plastic bags of gifts for Thenjie lumped around us.

A policeman in his teens sat on the reception counter toying with a dried flower bouquet of proteas, their centers bulging like giant bee abdomens. "He was doing nothing, just nothing," Thamie later said. "And paid to do it."

Four women prisoners followed by two matrons were marched out the door to a two-story block of apartments where the families of police lived.

"What are they doing?"

"They use prisoners to clean their houses," Reebs told me.

Reebs had been Thenjie's cellmate at the Fort prison in 1978. She had become involved in politics at the University of the North in much the same way as had Thenjie at Fort Hare.

After a short wait in the prison lobby, our parcels were accepted, although the head of the prison warned us not to bring food the next time; the regulations did not allow it.

"The major is not so bad," Thamie whispered, speaking of the head of the prison. He, like all police, has a military-style rank. "He speaks Xhosa."

Reebs and I waited while Thamie and Lumumba entered an adjacent room. The door between was left open.

Thamie held Lumumba on her lap. They had to shout to be heard through the thick plastic window. A black guard who spoke Xhosa stood behind Thenjie to monitor the conversation. But the women shouted to each other in English about news of friends and news in the papers.

"Pretoria is worried about the missing millions," Thamie yelled through the plastic, referring to a government funds scandal.

"Ya, and they will forget about the missing people in prisons," Thenjie shouted back.

Reebs, sitting beside me, suddenly kicked off her shoes and sank to the floor. "Watch," she whispered, indicating the area where the matrons might appear. She crawled to the open door of Thamie's cubicle, poked her head inside, looked up, and waved.

Thenjie did not falter in her conversation.

Reebs crept back to the bench. Clearly, I was next. I slid to the floor and traced her path. Easing my head into the cubicle, I peered up. Thenjie continued shouting to Thamie but smiled. I crawled back to the bench.

"She looks good," Reebs concluded.

After forty-five minutes, the matron ordered Thenjie back to her cell, which amounted to solitary confinement because there were no other women political prisoners in Potchefstroom.

The next day was Thenjie's birthday. She would be twenty-eight.

THE

LIBERAL

SPECTRUM

Helen Suzman in her garden in Johannesburg

13

Using Parliament

If we had deliberately set out to produce a criminal society, we couldn't have done better than this country.
—*Helen Suzman, 1978*

I n 1978 the United Nations honored Martin Luther King, Jr., and Helen Suzman for their defense of human rights.

A member of the Progressive Federal Party (PFP), Helen Suzman has been in South Africa's Parliament since 1953. She represents and leads the English-speaking, highly educated whites, whose power is exercised in corporate board rooms and through the opposition press. She has managed to defend both the oppressed blacks and the tax interests of her rich, white constituency in Houghton. She has outlasted prime ministers, Broederbond chairmen, heads of security police, cabinet ministers, and, most recently, disgraced, former Prime Minister John Vorster, whose dour, "upside-down smile" she imitated for me with hilarious effect.

For many of her years in Parliament in the 1960s, Helen Suzman stood alone in her attack on apartheid legislation, a reminder that liberalism is but a narrow ribbon threaded through the white society. Often, whites glance around furtively before whispering, "I'm a Prog." They feel they are divulging shocking information. Such instances illustrate why Helen Suzman, a conservative by Western standards, is considered a radical by most South African whites. Few are neutral about her. To some young ones she is a heroine both for her stand and for her style, a quick and witty tongue and a combative humor that have spiced up many a plodding Parliamentary debate.

Thenjie has already voiced her opposition to Helen's political position. On November 25, 1977, almost exactly when Helen was trying to visit Thenjie in the Fort, *The Star* newspaper ran a full-page ad from the PFP. In huge letters it began: "It's a lie! Our opponents say that the Progressive Federal Party stands for black majority rule.

This is a lie. This is *swart gevaar* (black peril) propaganda of the worst kind—the evil which breaks down race relations and damages South Africa."

Neither the PFP nor the National Party wants universal suffrage. Whatever their political differences, they oppose universal suffrage for the same reason: in any election, blacks would outnumber whites. Helen describes the PFP's goal as "power-sharing with blacks."

The struggle for power between black nationalists and the Afrikaner rulers does not take place in Parliament. Blacks have no representation there. And the Afrikaners maneuver in secret: their Broederbond-approved plans are rubber-stamped into law by the National Party, which dominates Parliament.

However, over the years Helen Suzman has used Parliament as an arena to voice dissent. "The minutes record my vote against every bit of oppressive legislation this country ever introduced," she said. "It's a good feeling to know that."

I interviewed Helen in the gracious, expensive Hyde Park suburb where she lives. I walked through trees and flowers, down a curving asphalt driveway to her home on Melville Road.

Small, almost delicate, Helen speaks quickly, forcefully, accentuating her own political acumen.

I asked how she had fared all these years in Parliament as a woman and a member of the opposition party.

"Nationalists are ugly sometimes," she said, "especially these days . . . telling me how old I've become and how my charm has vanished. They think that will cut me to the quick. Little do they know I don't give a damn what they think of me or my charms now or twenty years ago. They're very crude."

"Have you had any flak because you're Jewish?"

"Oh, much flak. But I must say, less now than ten years ago. I put that down to Israel's Six Day War. They were so impressed by it. Nationalists who wouldn't greet me before, now stop me in the lobby of Parliament and give me a pat on the back, saying, 'Mooi skaat (good show), Helen.'"

When she asked them why they were suddenly praising her, they replied: "The war, the war."

"In the past," Helen said. "they told me to go back to Israel. Now they tell me to go back to Moscow, Israel's too good for me. Really, a decided change, but, of course, they are—as always—still insulting.

"They say, 'The honorable member's people (the Jews) are only interested in making money out of South Africa'—that sort of thing."

"Without the presence of blacks in Parliament, how do you include their needs?" I asked.

"I don't claim to speak for the blacks. I voice opinions I know are shared by black people and those opinions concern the pass laws, the Group Areas Act, and the lack of equal opportunity. But I don't necessarily share the same objectives as young black radicals. I can understand exactly what their motivation is: 'The hell with these bloody whites. They have been living off our backs. We will get what we can from them.' The people who are doing the pilfering— servants in white households—haven't gotten to the bomb-throwing stage yet, but it is a bomb-throwing thing, isn't it?"

"Are you in contact with many black people?" I asked.

"I have a few blacks I would number as friends," she said, "but not many, really. One is engaged in one's life and it's very difficult to get to blacks at night. That's the time when you really establish your social contacts if you're a working woman."

"What changes do you believe are necessary?" I asked, "and how would PFP bring them about?"

"There's got to be a redistribution of wealth," she said. "The present system is not conducive to lasting, peaceful race relations in this country. It doesn't mean I want a Marxist form of government. I have little faith, shall I say, in the freedom of the individual under a Marxist government.

"I believe the redistribution is going to take place, but through the use of a (limited) franchise (voting) system, and the development of trade unions. I don't want exclusively black unions, but mixed trade unions."

Helen Suzman has, over the years, consistently worked to expose the repressive functions of the South African police and prisons. She gave a recent account of how the police operate.

An eighty-year-old woman from Helen's constituency phoned her about releasing her servant from prison. The man had been pruning branches when police pulled him out of a tree, demanded his pass book and, without giving him a chance to produce it, beat him and carted him away in their van.

"None of them was in uniform," she said. "This is the way they prowl the northern suburbs. If we had deliberately set out to produce a criminal society, we couldn't have done better than this country. It is nurturing the most immoral society. How can you expect the children to have any sort of normal upbringing or sense of values?"

At the time of our interview, Helen was actively working against the Natal Code—a law that makes all black women permanent minors.

"You know, married South African women have a hell of a time with contractual obligations in community property. But black women have a much worse time, particularly those under the Natal

Code, who never attain majority and, indeed, when they marry become permanent minors.

"I've been to see (Zulu Chief) Gatsha Buthelezi over this; I've called him a male chauvinist and all sorts of things." She smiled. "Well, he denies being one, of course, old Gatsha. Anyway, the Kwa Zulu government appointed a commission of inquiry into the Natal Code and made some far-reaching recommendations for change. But, of course, it has to come through Parliament because the Natal Code is a South African government law.

"I've raised it in Parliament and said, 'Why don't we change this?' They say very piously, 'We don't like to interfere with the natives' customs, you see.' And I say, 'It's the first time I ever heard you worry about interfering with the black man; you do it in every other phase, why not this one?' 'Not until they ask for it,' they say. You see, it's almost a male conspiracy.

"I'm a feminist," Helen said. "But the force motivating my life is the broader issue of race. You must be a feminist because your feelings on racial issues have to do with injustice; and many injustices are meted out to women.

"The young, educated whites are in despair and leaving the country. I mean the English-speaking ones; very few Afrikaners leave. I don't see anything to galvanize white women into activity."

There are small groups of feminists in Cape Town, Johannesburg, and Pretoria. Now and then they publish *From Women*, a magazine frequently banned by the government.

In 1976 a national convention was held in Pretoria. More than two hundred women representing over fifty organizations attended and established the Women's Legal Status Committee, a middle-of-the-road organization. It outlined six problem areas: matrimonial property, divorce, women in employment, joint taxation, abortion reform, and the special problems of black women. However, the committee has since focused on only the first three. Black women would be little affected by any gains made.

(White women's lack of support for abortion reform is both racist and religious. It is black women who suffer severely from the abortion laws, since many whites can pay to obtain illegal abortions or can travel to London. Twenty women a day are admitted to Baragwanath hospital in Soweto for complications due to self-inflicted abortions. Admissions also reach thirty to forty a day at the "non-European" hospital in Johannesburg.)

In Parliament, Helen Suzman's outspoken defense of blacks is sometimes too liberal for the PFP, her own party, which has moved to the right.

"The party that had my heart and soul is no longer in existence," she said. "We're a different party now. We have merged twice. There are attitudes in the party now which make me feel I'm not a hundred percent at home anymore.

"That's the tragedy. That's why I can't see how progressive ideas are going to dominate the political scene. The young are leaving this country in droves. Everywhere I go—Dallas, Houston, Toronto, Boston, Los Angeles—I meet well-educated, well-trained, always progressively minded young whites from South Africa. They should be here, preparing to take the place of people like me."

"Do you think about the future here?" I asked.

"I suppose South Africa will follow the Zimbabwean model . . . a prolonged war . . ."

"Why do you go on?" I asked.

"This is the question I ask myself every day—why go on? I must be out of my tiny mind," she said. "You keep on because while you are living here you can't do nothing about it. Really, you can't, unless you're the type who can put on blinkers and go play golf or lie beside the pool or just shop all day long."

Sheena Duncan

14

The Black Sash

Is White

The best method is not to look higher than anybody's knees but just keep my eyes down. That way, passers-by can get no reaction from me. —*Black Sash member, 1978*

T he woman speaking in the quote above is white. The harassment being avoided is from white South African men who curse, jeer, and use long hat pins. The situation described was a lonely vigil in 1978 against apartheid in Port Elizabeth, the car-manufacturing city on the Indian Ocean, where Steve Biko was detained the last time.

More than twenty years ago, thousands of white women, with black sashes draped over their shoulders, marched to protest the desecration of individual rights by the ruling National Party. White gloves, fitted hats, sensible shoes with prim, feet-together stance, they stood vigil and sang songs. They were the Black Sash women.

Established in 1956, the Black Sash soon reached a peak of ten thousand members. This was in the early 1960s when Mrs. Minsky, the unknown woman who Thenjie deduced must have been a member of Black Sash, gave money for Thenjie's school fees to her mother.

But by 1980, Sash membership had dwindled to eleven hundred, and to be a member was considered by whites to be more radical than belonging to the PFP. On January 5, 1981, a Black Sash member, Esther Levitan of Johannesburg, was detained briefly without charge by the police.

Seldom are white women, especially fifty-five-year-old white women like Mrs. Levitan, detained, for the Black Sash has bent over backward not to break the laws of the land. Almost all Sash women are English-speaking. They are not anticapitalist.

Sheena Duncan, former Sash president, remains an active worker in the organization. Her mother founded Black Sash, then nursed it through the 1960s when support waned and whites moved to the right.

Sheena's home is in the upper-middle-class suburb of Park-hurst. A magnificent garden rolls up a slant of land in the back. Two untrimmed poodles cavorted on the lawn while Sheena served tea on her patio. Sheena's husband is an architect. Her two daughters, like herself, were educated at Rhodene, an English private school for girls in Johannesburg.

Sheena's contact with the black community occurs mainly in the Sash advice offices, where blacks are assisted through the maze of pass laws. In her resonant voice she speaks against apartheid with a precision and authority that profoundly irritate the government.

"The advice office made me understand what the political system means to the people," Sheena said. "I'm not boasting, but outside of Sash, nobody in this country—except the government's black affairs department—understands that the pass laws and all that goes with them are the foundation, the cornerstone, of the whole structure.

"The citizenship thing, where blacks are stripped of South African citizenship and assigned to homelands, is much worse than blacks think it is," Sheena emphasized.

"Sash has a broad vision of the system because of its day-to-day work at the advice offices. Almost no lawyers understand it; they never handle these cases."

I spent a day with Sheena in the Johannesburg advice office. She sat at a small table where blacks came for help. At her side, a black woman translated.

How to obtain pensions; how to transfer a house to a child; how to get one's name on the twenty-two-thousand–person waiting list for a house in Soweto—these were some of the problems. A man from the Tswana tribe wanted to spell his name differently and be reclassified a Zulu in order to avoid carrying a Bophuthatswana passport, which deprived him of rights in the white area. Generally, Sheena directed them to a particular government office.

Wherever Sash opens an advice office, whites in the building complain about the poor and illiterate who come to seek help. Men with flapping earlobes from which tribal disc earrings were removed; women with sweeping Zulu bonnets needing help because husbands have deserted them; schoolboys having difficulty obtaining first pass books. When unemployment goes up or the government passes a new decree, the advice office becomes even busier.

"We have been overwhelmed since legislation (in 1979) introduced a fine of 500 rands (then $575) for an employer of an unregistered worker," Sheena explained. "Now there will be no illegal work. Thousands and thousands of families have been entirely dependent on such employment." (The heavy tax on employers was a promptly adopted recommendation of the Riekert Commission, a government-appointed body that focused on Section 10 of the Bantu Consolidation Act of 1945, which controls movement of blacks from homelands into the urban areas of the country. Although the commission mouthed the "free enterprise" concept of every man being able to sell his labor wherever he wishes, in fact, the entire thrust of the study was that "influx control," or control of the flow of blacks, must be strengthened, with the unemployed being forced back to the tribal homelands.)

"Many whites say, 'What difference does it make if the homelands are called independent countries? It's just a different piece of paper blacks must carry.' But there's a tremendous difference. If a Tswana, for example, buys a house in Soweto and leaves it to his child, the child can inherit the lease, but not the right to occupy the house. He can apply for permission—which is different from having a legal right. The government can refuse permission, take away the house, and force the urban black to move to a rural homeland. He would lose his Section 10 rights and be given Section 12 rights, which makes him a foreigner in white areas."

Sheena described her argument about citizenship laws with the businessmen in the Urban Foundation (established after the 1976 uprisings by a group of the country's largest corporations to defuse further black protest by building an urban black middle class as a buffer).

"For the first time, big business is cooperating actively with the government," Sheena said. "Until now their support of the system was apathetic. They were content as long as they made their profit. The government is attempting to have a black middle class support the status quo by awarding privileges to the 'qualified.' There are distinct signs they may succeed.

"There's a glossy pamphlet called *Johannesburg* produced here by the advertising firm J. Walter Thompson. When you look at it, you would not believe you were living in the same society. It's all part of a big support operation to encourage foreign investment. And Western journalists don't try to uncover the truth. It has become impossible to talk to the white community. They are all lit up about 'change.' And now business is very sympathetic to (Prime Minister) Botha; they are not one bit alarmed at power being concentrated in fewer and fewer hands. All this at the expense of the majority, and I am very depressed."

"Why hasn't the government banned Black Sash?" I asked.

"They don't think we're effective enough to worry about because we're women. We're immune because we're unequal. It's the Calvinist definition of women. It's almost impossible for a member of the National Party or the Dutch Reformed Church to take any woman seriously. The Broederbond is entirely male. Women's lack of equality in that particular society is extraordinary. South African whites are taught right through their lives—in school, in university—that women like us are dishonest, communist, whatever.

"I tell the Nationalist Afrikaner that such and such a law means black men working in Johannesburg see their wives only once a year. If the Afrikaner is tolerant, he might reply: 'We are aware of that, but you know the government is doing tremendous things to introduce fast commuter transport.' But when we talk to someone in the railways and find out what it costs to shift workers a couple of hundred kilometers, we know it's a pipe dream—a pipe dream the Afrikaner media put across continuously as truth. Even if they admit the breakup of the African family exists and is wrong, they say it's a question of time and will be corrected."

"What about the English-speaking white?" I asked.

"Just as bad. I had an argument with a good, well-meaning Rotarian man whose firm has done a lot about training workers, getting schooling for their children, and so on. He said, 'But you can't seriously say there should be no influx control.'

"I said, 'Look, you come from Cape Town. If you were black, you wouldn't be allowed in Johannesburg. Are you prepared to accept that sort of control?' And he said, 'Oh, but it wouldn't happen because there are always exemptions for people with skills.'

"It's very hard to make people know and understand the truth. They have no dealings with black people."

After the 1976 Soweto protests, Black Sash experienced a small increase in its membership, but many more women joined the more conservative, multiracial organization, Women for Peace, established in September 1976. The organization disavows political aims. Its purpose: to ameliorate friction between the races. Toward this end, it sponsors social gatherings and makes occasional presentations on issues to government officials.

"People see Women for Peace as a safer way to act," Sheena said, "because they made it clear that politics was not their thing."

"I have heard whites accuse the Sash of being abrasive, brash, and harming race relations in South Africa," I said.

"Propaganda about Black Sash has always been that we were

radical, militant, neo-communist. I wish Sash were as strong, aggressive, and abrasive as people seem to think we are. People don't realize how much information they wouldn't have if the Sash had gone out of existence. Twenty-three years of water dripping on stone, just to put out the facts.

"Sometimes I think . . . if only one could expose the policy, the corruption, that goes right through from top to bottom. But it's almost impossible.

"The white society believes that when the government policy unfolds everything will be okay. It is incredible, even *verligte* Afrikaners think only of different boundaries for homelands, more consolidation, more land—that kind of jazz. I haven't heard anyone within Nationalist circles say we've got to rethink the whole policy."

"What about less-educated blacks? How do they resist apartheid?" I asked.

"When Transkei became independent in 1976, the militancy of blacks was very high. We used to have people tearing up their papers and saying, 'I won't, I won't.' But you've got to be very brave to defy the pass laws, because you can't work; you would spend the rest of your life in fear of being arrested. You can't do anything without that identity document."

We sat at a small garden table in the shade of the house. It was January and summer. Sheena poured another cup of tea.

"The churches are enough to break your heart—the church establishment," she said.

"You hear sound statements from bishops and moderators, but their authority is so weak, and the church structure so heavy; it never gets any further. They don't have a sense of urgency about what is happening in the black community, particularly among young people."

Sheena noted that Christianity is deeply rooted in Soweto, with parents forcing their children to attend church and raising them to respect ministers. Yet, now, the teen-agers are rejecting religion for political reasons.

"The Black Consciousness people are Christian; and they seem concerned about the youngsters. Maybe we are seeing the last generation of black Christian leaders," Sheena said.

"I think the criticism by young blacks that Christianity props up the system is correct. The church supports all sorts of militaristic functions in our society. This praying for the 'boys on the border' (soldiers). I'm not saying they don't need our prayers. But in white churches, there is no suggestion that blacks on the other side of the border are also our Christian young."

Citing church blessing of regimental flags, Sheena said, "In a sense, we're already in a wartime situation. I was a child during the Second World War. But I remember the glamour of uniforms . . . Vera Lynn . . . the whole scene. You just have to listen to those radio programs on SABC—Pat Carr and 'Forces Request'—and hear the sort of messages girlfriends and parents are sending: 'We're so proud of you, son.'"

Sheena, a confirmed pacifist, had been convinced that Afrikaner Nationalists would be susceptible to charges of Christian immorality because apartheid contravened the Bible. Now she believes that assumption was wrong.

She belongs to the Anglican Church's Justice and Reconciliation Committee and the South African Council of Churches (SACC). In her work for the SACC's Family, Home and Life Division, she has begun to set up advice centers, similar to those of Sash, in churches around the country.

Since the 1977 banning of Beyers Naudé's Christian Institute, SACC has become the organized "left" that contains whites and blacks. The ruling Afrikaners detest SACC. So far, SACC's ties with foreign churches and the World Council of Churches has protected it from outright suppression.

Still, a few liberals remain concerned that the government will cut off SACC's overseas funds. Its two-million-dollar budget provides legal defense for detainees and assists the unemployed as well as the families of banned and detained people.

Sheena fears a cutoff of SACC's overseas money would wipe out the organization because very little money and support come from the local white churches.

"What would you do?" I asked.

"I, and others I know, would immediately join in a confessing church—the Bonhoeffer idea. There's a lot of talk about it now, but it's not urgent yet because work is still being done in SACC."

(In 1933, Dietrich Bonhoeffer, a German theologian, publicly denounced Hitler and abandoned the safety of the United States to return to Germany and work for the "Confessing Church." After two years in prison, where he wrote letters explaining his stand, he was hanged in 1945.)

"Why is it called the 'confessing church'?"

"I don't know; I think it was the German terminology. It is a sort of back-to-the-catacomb, an underground church which declares, 'We cannot cooperate with the government; we are going to stand firm as Christians and go wherever our belief takes us.'"

In 1979, SACC members made a policy decision to apply the conscience principle and called on Christians not to request permits to enter black areas, but to go into them in civil disobedience.

I asked why Black Sash has never advocated civil disobedience since it originated as a protest group.

"One of the earliest national conference resolutions was that Black Sash would protest by all lawful means. That decision was made at a time when it was perfectly possible to do what they wanted by lawful means. In those days, they could have mass marches, ten abreast. Look at some of the old photographs. . . .

"Today, mass action is illegal, an act of civil disobedience, which is a philosophical concept not taught in the schools of South Africa. A lot of people think the only kind of protest remaining is what Margaret Nash did at a black squatter camp in Cape Town. She placed her body in front of a bulldozer which was razing black people's shacks. The police carried her off.

"The trouble is we're so tiny that the police come back the next day and we don't have enough time to get the message across. I'm sorry there aren't more white South Africans protesting publicly. We might not be in such a mess."

"Aren't whites afraid?" I asked.

"Among the Nationalists, I don't put fear as high as I used to. They are sure of their power; they have lost the old insecurity of living in extreme poverty, competing for jobs with the black man.

"But there's an inculcated fear of blacks. Every black man in the street is suspected of being a drunk or intent on rape, unless he happens to be someone you know."

The fear, Sheena explained, is fueled by the government.

"Cabinet ministers keep warning the people it's absolutely essential to have their workers registered.

"Everything is a 'security measure,' and the apartheid policy is as firm as ever."

Ina Perlman

15

The Institute

Remains

Concerned

It's the white defending the indefensible. You saw it with the Portuguese in Mozambique; you saw it with the Americans in Vietnam. *—Ina Perlman, 1979*

To Afrikaner nationalists, the Institute of Race Relations denounces apartheid at a time when the country is organizing for war unity, or what the government calls "total onslaught"; therefore, it is subversive.

To black nationalists such as Thenjie, the institute does not aid but perhaps delays the revolution.

Ina Perlman is regional secretary of the Institute of Race Relations, a research organization founded in 1929. The institute has worked toward conveying to the white society an understanding of the situation of blacks. It is the oldest of the liberal organizations and, unlike Black Sash, is not a protest group.

Ina is devoted to the goals of the institute and tries to fight creeping conservatism within it. Her devotion is emotional, based on personal relationships. Most white South Africans decry emotion, think it is not a good thing, and try to suppress it—even when they cannot. Ina unsettles such whites by personifying what is best about this research body: the human reaction to the cold, printed word.

Ina, who is taking Zulu lessons and who learned Afrikaans from her nanny as a child in Bloemfontein, is like a periscope peering over the society. She is in touch, more than any other person I met, with all sides.

Ina has never met Thenjie but she knew about her detentions. She knew other activists in the Black Consciousness Movement and related the story of one, Dimza Pityana, who worked for the institute in Port Elizabeth, was banned, then fled to London with her daughter and husband, Barney Pityana, who was Steve Biko's second in command in the movement.

"We had lunch together at our Durban conference," Ina said. "Dimza had come out of her first detention. I expected the bitterness and standoffishness to have increased, but it had all gone. During lunch, a big, fat fool, a minister, sat himself next to us and said to Dimza, 'Was it bad? Tell us all about it.'

"Dimza started talking and I must say . . ." Ina shook her head, frowning. "She told the story of sixty-five days without changing her clothes, of being interrogated for something like sixty hours nonstop. They used to interrogate her, having her squat. Can you imagine how exhausting that was? Squatting in the middle of the floor, not allowed to touch anything.

"The only time they became more decent was when she could see herself moving out of herself. Apparently she had started screaming and screaming and screaming. She said they never hit her. After that they behaved a bit better.

"She was in solitary. They wouldn't allow her sanitary towels [napkins]. They brought her clothes the last four days of the sixty-eight days she was held," Ina said. "They took her Bible away; they said she was a communist so she had no need for it.

"I said to her, 'Dimza.' I think I just said, 'Dimza.' She said to me, 'You know, looking back at it, I don't resent it because it gave me the opportunity to find myself as a person.' "

Ina, whose agnostic father insisted on a formal Jewish religious education for her and who made her read the New Testament "because you must live among these people and know how they think," follows the Afrikaner side of South Africa as assiduously as she does the black.

Until security police killed it, she monitored the Koinonia protest group, a *verligte* Dutch Reformed organization opposed to the Immorality Act and based at the university of Potchesfstroom. She knows tidbits of information which she slips into her conversation, revealing insights into the Afrikaner psychology. Ina gave an example of an unusual Afrikaner, a Mr. Fouche, who insists on living in Soweto, the last white to remain there after apartheid decreed the races must live separately.

"This Fouche is a character," Ina said. "The young blacks despise him, but they don't touch him. He sponsors about eight black kids through school; virtually his entire salary goes to them. On a Monday you can't visit him because he sponsors a soccer team, the Pimville Pups, which always loses.

"He's a great administrator: he is a paternalistic Afrikaner. Look, he's a supremely just man, not corrupt," Ina explained. "He knows his law, but he's the father."

"Does he support apartheid?" I asked.

"Oh, I'm sure he believes in apartheid. His attitude toward blacks is they are his property, which is why he has to give them a good deal. That's *me volk* (my people). It's no accident the Afrikaner refers to his farm labor as *me volk*," Ina said.

"On the farm . . . you know the way Americans would talk about the pickaninnies? Here, there is a song at the harvest feast that says, *die volkies*. The diminutive is used for blacks. But *die volk* is the Afrikaners."

Ina knows the geography of Soweto well. She can tell you where the first police shot was fired in 1976; she knows the locations of the various confrontations; she is familiar with the high schools that produced the most militant student protestors.

She knew as early as March 1976 that trouble was brewing in Soweto over the use of Afrikaans in the black schools and she pushed the institute to warn the government long before June 16, 1976, that conflict could result. The government did nothing.

The institute is best known for its *Annual Survey of Race Relations*. The survey compiles statistics and records political and economic events and facts from newspapers, government publications, and other sources. The information gathered is published in book form and serves as a basic resource for research and reference.

In 1948 Afrikaners set up the South African Bureau of Racial Affairs (SABRA) to displace the Institute of Race Relations. Money formerly allocated to the institute from local authorities was diverted to SABRA, according to a reliable source. However, SABRA never gained the institute's credibility internationally.

For years the institute's annual budget of 400,000 rands ($460,000) has been supplemented by funds from such American foundations as Rockefeller, Ford, Carnegie, and Phelps-Stokes, all of which Afrikaners consider left-wing.

Ina believes that criticism of the institute by blacks is valid. She admits the institute does not attempt to formulate political strategies from its research, nor does it challenge the government so much as irritate it. However, in South Africa even that requires fortitude.

"Whatever I do is aboveboard," she said. "I've had one slightly threatening call from the security police. I haven't gotten involved in party politics. Look, if the institute doesn't last, South Africa is a complete dictatorship."

Ina is in her mid-forties. She lives with her family in Northcliff, in the same suburb as Gabrielle Malan. Her home is set on a rocky hill with a swimming pool in the garden below.

I visited her at home and in her office and accompanied her to Soweto's Naledi, a transit camp for old, indigent blacks whom the government planned to send to homelands.

Before becoming regional secretary in 1974, Ina was a volunteer worker in Soweto. She saw the poverty and despair as well as the rising anger. The institute warned the government to respond to Soweto's demands, but the government did not.

"I'm distressed at the high threshold of resistance to cries for help. Did you see the *Post* story of people scavenging for food in Soweto's rubbish dumps? A few years ago someone would have stepped in to organize something. Now, it's just another sob story.

"What can I do?" she said. "What else can I do? It seems hopeless, but I don't believe in violence. I can't support violence."

Ina's despair is not rooted in a superficial overview of the present society. She has a clear, historical perspective.

"It's the white defending the indefensible. You saw it with the Portuguese in Mozambique; you saw it with the Americans in Vietnam.

"A lot of white South Africans have a sneaking suspicion they are wrong. I don't for a minute think the Platteland (rural) Afrikaner is convinced. Isn't this one of the things with Calvinism? It has the most rigid right-and-wrong code of all religions: no compromise, you know. Their great split with the Anglicans and Lutherans was because those groups compromised. So the Calvinist must never compromise.

"The minute Afrikaners stand up against apartheid, they are outcasts. Look how many of them have scuttled back in. It's only your top, top-caliber people, like the banned head of the Christian Institute, Beyers Naudé. Look at what happened to him. But he's an exceptional man.

"Fred Van Wyk (Afrikaner head of the institute at the time) is the same. His wife supported him, but she resents the ostracism, resents being pushed into it all. He was an elder in the Dutch Reformed Church and he was axed."

Ina, who said she's been in liberal women's organizations for "donkeys years," reminisced about her volunteer work in Soweto with the African Feeding Program.

"The thing that used to bug me was the white lady bountifuls coming out to the Africans; some used to bring boxes of tissues to wipe snotty noses.

"But the attitude of the African Self-Help Program was quite different. The white women were there to do the jobs African women couldn't do."

Ina began volunteer work in 1960 in Sophiatown, which was later demolished and turned into a white suburb named Triomphe. She then moved to work in Shelters, the squatters' camp where Thenjie was born and where she was tended by an old woman who drank and ate her food while her mother worked.

"We used to bring peanut butter to Shelters, help the families with their banking. We ran a sewing group. Somebody evolved a marvelous pattern for changing slacks into skirts because at that time African women didn't wear slacks.

"It was there I learned that the minute you tell people something's good for them, you build up resistance. You've got to do it gently. There was a fabulous fortified skim milk they used in displaced persons' camps in Europe. Eleanor Ponsonby from the Duke of Devonshire's family—typical English—decided Africans must have this milk and we practically had a riot. They wouldn't have it."

On the wall in Ina's home were large paintings done by Africans, one of Pimville, Soweto, where she did volunteer work in 1960. I admired an old, ornate tea wagon nearby.

"That was my mother's," Ina said. "She brought it out of Germany in 1922—part of her trousseau. During the war I used to have a fit if my mother spoke German on the street." Ina's grandfather on her father's side emigrated from Germany in 1860 and owned a store in Potchefstroom.

Although many Afrikaners are anti-Semitic and supported Hitler, the present attitude is one of cooperation between South Africa and Israel. This includes an exchange of military expertise and other strategic aid.

"I cannot bear the way the Jewish community here makes no stand," Ina said. "They are so terrified of being victimized because they remember the Hitler cry that Jews were liberals.

"This is the thing that terrifies me most about South Africa: the constant parallel with Germany."

She believes that social anti-Semitism has never been as marked in South Africa as it was in the United States or England, even though there are still golf clubs where no Jew is admitted. "By and large, the Jewish community here is like the American, but probably freer.

"Chauvinism is a terrible thing, even when it's your own group's chauvinism," she said.

Ina's children were sent to a Catholic private school rather than a Jewish one because she wanted to expose them to different ways of thinking in order to "enable them to question." She had removed them from public schools after the Nationalist government introduced its Christian National Education program into the curriculum.

"The older I become, the more I believe the Jesuit thing. I don't believe the first seven years, but if you have a person for the first fourteen years of his life you haven't a hope in hell of changing his attitudes."

Ina and her nineteen-year-old son John agree politically more often than the rest of the family. After John finishes his university degree, he must decide whether he will flee the country, serve in the army, or face six years in prison if he refuses.

"People are starving in South Africa and whites are not aware," John said. "They're numb. The first person to fall out of a building while in detention was front page news. Now such people rate a column on the third page, unless it was someone important."

At a braai (cookout) around the pool, John told his father, who is a surgeon and was then president of a local Rotary chapter, he did not like the latest brochure about South Africa that the Rotary was circulating to chapters in the United States. "It has half-true information," he said.

"Yes," Ina agreed. "It said black wages had increased at a high percentage, but didn't add the gap between blacks and whites had also increased."

"How do you explain most whites' attitudes?" I asked Ina at another time.

"This is the country of the ostrich," she said. "The natural habitat. You don't have to go any further. The ostrich sticks its head in the sand. A middle class that's got everything to lose will try to do anything to stop the revolution—even if it goes against their own consciences. The easiest way to live is by not thinking."

Ina, who once told me, "What I do is a drop in the ocean," has not chosen the easy path. She thinks and acts and worries and worries.

Mary Benson

16

Banned but

Undaunted

Exile is very, very painful. I often think South Africans
have a peculiar anguish to their exile; something about the
people left behind. Whenever I went back to South Africa,
I felt the energy, joy, giftedness of the great mass of black
people that has been systematically kept down.
                                                    —*Mary Benson, 1979*

"It was a terrible wrench to come away from South
Africa, to become a prohibited immigrant; but
friends believed . . . and I came to believe . . . I could
do more for the struggle abroad."

Mary Benson, fourth-generation South African, put under house
arrest in 1965, went into exile in 1966.

She now lives in London "away from my beloved people, sun,
and space." She is gray-haired and resilient, a writer whose work has
been banned and cannot be quoted in South Africa.

The books she has written contradict the belief of some that the
struggle against apartheid has just begun. In particular, her book
South Africa: A Struggle for a Birthright contains the seminal history
of early black protest.

Mary lives a solitary life on not very much money, but she has
many friends and continues to do what she can for people, particularly people in trouble with the South African authorities.

During the 1930s, when she was twenty-five, Mary dreamed of
being a movie star and went from her home in Pretoria to Holly-
wood.

"While I was crossing America in a Greyhound bus, a black man
sat beside me and I was furious at his 'cheek.' That's an example of
my racial attitudes at the time.

"Before my attitudes changed, living in South Africa had been

155

terribly boring, centered on the country club. I couldn't wait to go abroad. When I began to meet blacks and Indians and went to their homes, I experienced their tremendous generosity, energy, and liveliness. It became a new world. Suddenly I felt sorry for all those whites who had absolutely no idea, who were stuck in their dreadful, mean, materialistic world."

She spoke of two white men who contributed to her political conversion and commitment. "They made me feel profoundly about my country."

One was Athol Fugard, the Afrikaner playwright who lives in Port Elizabeth.

"He was everything I'd been brought up to feel snobbish about: this terrible accent, grubby fingernails, and he and his family working as stewards on the railways. My family were rather high in the administration of railways."

Mary visited Athol and his wife, Sheila, in the early 1960s. She discovered and wrote about dozens of "terrible trials in the Eastern Cape," and went "from one dreadful little courtroom to another in all these dorps where none of the accuseds' families were allowed in."

Mary wrote *At the Still Point,* a novel about the Cape trials. When she told Donald Woods, editor of *The Daily Dispatch* in East London, about the trials, he "wasn't interested." He was busy decorating his office.

"The trials still go on," Mary said, "and no one is writing about them. One can't seem to break through with the whole story."

The other person who greatly influenced her was Bram Fischer, the Afrikaner lawyer and communist leader who became sick in prison and died. His lifelong fight against apartheid made him the only white man whom many blacks look upon as a hero, as Steve Biko confirmed. For years he had worked alongside blacks, taking the same risks.

Mary had never known a communist before 1961, when she became secretary for the Treason Fund Trial in Pretoria.

"I'd been rather petrified of communists, terrified of how they might use what I said. But I came to know them and their incredible generosity. I saw how deeply the African people trusted them."

In the same year, while she was working on the history of the African National Congress (ANC), her friendship with Bram Fischer began and for a brief time she lived with his wife and son.

Two years later, during the Rivonia trial of Nelson Mandela, Walter Sisulu, and other ANC leaders, "I went off to the United Nations to lobby on behalf of these men whom I had come to know and respect.

"Bram was against people being singled out as individuals. I used to argue a bit about it, saying, for most people to learn about a situation . . . and to feel it . . . they must come through it by way of other human beings. He felt this was making the struggle too personal a thing.

"Later, when Bram himself was put on trial for being a communist along with, I think, thirteen others, he decided he would have to go underground to continue the struggle no matter what the cost. He was able to evade the police most of that year.

"I was in South Africa and met him regularly; I think very few of his own party people were around. I valued all our time together. He was a very great man, and my very close friend.

"He had a brilliant disguise; no one could possibly have known him. He'd shaved his head bald, dyed his mustache auburn, changed glasses, and become slim. He had encounters with people who'd known him, including a senior police officer, but they never recognized him.

"The police kept detaining other people, made them stand day after day until they broke someone and found out where Bram was staying; that November, he was captured.

"There had been a lot of criticism of him for going underground. He was heartbroken by the law association's repudiation, their judgment that it was dishonest of him to leave his own trial. In fact, before he went underground, while still on trial, he was given permission to go to London for a privy council court case, which he had won.

"In London, leading British politicians said to him, 'Why on earth don't you stay?' He knew, going back, he was likely to be imprisoned. But he said, 'I gave my word that I would return.'

"So going underground really was a great sacrifice for him. There was no, absolutely no, opposition left in South Africa in 1965. Everyone had been worn down through detention and torture. He felt there was no justice, and he was acting for a higher form of justice by trying to keep the struggle alive.

"In court, after he was captured and sentenced to life imprisonment, he made a very clear statement about his commitment. Essentially, he said, what motivated him was being an Afrikaner, being deeply aware of how blacks felt about Afrikaners, and feeling the appalling responsibility Afrikaners have for all that has been done to blacks in South Africa.

"His death showed what incredible hatred Afrikaners have for one of their own who reneges—the way they insisted on taking his ashes back to prison. You know he had cancer and was terribly ill in a very short time. They refused all the appeals and protests from around the world to let him go to any of his family. Finally it was too late for him to even enjoy seeing his one grandchild.

"And, then, after the funeral, the family was made to give back the ashes.

"I continued doing the research for the ANC history, although I didn't think I was the person to write it. But there was no one else.

"I met secretly with ANC leader Nelson Mandela several times to interview him while he was underground."

He went underground in 1960, after Sharpeville, when virtually all opposition people were arrested—thousands, black and white.

"Mandela was the first leader to function as an organizer from underground. He was extraordinary, very strong, a great sense of humor, very handsome. He toured the African states, studied military tactics in Algeria, and came up to London. He was captured in, I think, August 1962. It was a miracle he wasn't gotten much sooner because he's huge and his disguise, when I saw him, was a chauffeur's white coat and peaked cap.

"On one occasion we drove through Johannesburg, with me as the madam in the back seat. The car began coughing and spluttering. I was terrified it would break down and he would be recognized. He had some very narrow escapes.

"Meanwhile, the period of armed struggle began. Sabotage had broken out. ANC leader Chief Albert Luthuli was awarded the Nobel Peace Prize. Walter Sisulu, another ANC leader, came to Johannesburg and asked me to rush down to Natal and help Luthuli because press people from all over the world were turning up.

"That was really extraordinary. I mean, the permit I was issued said I agreed not to interfere in the private affairs of the 'Bantu'; that I agreed not to talk politics with the 'Bantu.'

"When Luthuli went off to Oslo, I went around South Africa talking to whomever I could about the history of ANC. I wrote my notes in code and mailed them to myself in England, where, after fifteen months, I returned to work on the book.

"Now my work is mostly historical: a life of Mandela, a radio documentary play of Robben Island, and so on.

"But while I was still in South Africa the police followed me everywhere, more interested in the people I was meeting than in myself. They were concerned about my association with Chief Luthuli. They wrote about it in one of the Afrikaner newspapers.

"Anyhow, I went to live in London, where I had done lobbying, lecturing, and writing for some time past. But one very soon feels out of touch, however much there is a continual coming and going of friends and information from South Africa.

"Exile is very, very painful. I often think South Africans have a peculiar anguish to their exile; something about the people left behind. Whenever I went back to South Africa, I felt the energy, joy, giftedness of the great mass of black people that has been systematically kept down.

"In exile you manage to keep your pain under control; you do what little jobs you can when anything crops up; but it all seems inadequate and far off. Now and then, something very small breaks through and you're knocked out with it all over again: fresh feelings of the awfulness of leaving, of jealousy of people who can go in."

Mary Benson, who admired and felt close to the communist Bram Fischer, who describes Helen Suzman as "the outstanding member of Parliament for intellect and courage," still agrees with black nationalists that liberals are irrelevant to the struggle.

"Liberals," she said, "often function through sentimental and not sufficiently sensible, analytic motives."

"Should they halt their activities?" I asked.

"No, because it's your only life on this earth. In it you try to do what you can where you can."

Linda Bernhardt

17

Willing to

Share

The white man's protection of his white woman: this has a lot to do with the putting down of the black man.
—Linda Bernhardt, 1978

I n South Africa a white man almost invariably considers it flattering to be called a male chauvinist. He doesn't smile, however, when he is called a racist. He claims he is not. He makes the claim with great assurance.

Frantz Fanon, a black man born in Martinique, wrote in his book *Black Skin, White Masks*: "Out of the blackest part of my soul, across the zebra striping of my mind, surges this desire to be suddenly white . . .

"Now . . . who but a white woman can do this for me? By loving me she proves that I am worthy of white love. I am loved like a white man."

In South Africa the books of Fanon—and many others—are banned. Those young white people who do not *feel* comfortable with apartheid are denied the benefit of others' experiences. They must find their own way to understand the emotional ingredients of their society's racism.

Few white South African women wish to flout any of racism's deep taboos, particularly the one against loving a black man.

Cecille did. She loved a black activist she met at a university. "My friends helped me. I folded myself inside the boot of a car and they sneaked me into the township to be with him."

Harriet did. She lives in a white area with their two-year-old child and stays inside her apartment most of the time—away from society's open condemnation. She considers herself married, although she is not. The man she loves lives in Soweto, except when he can slip into the white area to be with her.

Linda did. Harriet and Cecille are pseudonyms. Linda is not. But before we get to Linda let me tell a story that will lead back to her.

In 1976, black leaders from all over the subcontinent arrived in Botswana to celebrate the tenth anniversary of independence. Many journalists attended.

However, there was not room at the Holiday Inn for everyone. Having secured sleeping space at a Peace Corps office, I walked around in the hallway asking about a ride to town. A black Foreign Minister overheard and said, "You can stay in my room." He gave me the key.

I lugged my suitcase and typewriter into his room. A short while later, the Foreign Minister knocked on the door, then entered. We discussed my state of weariness. He suggested a hot shower and bed. Leaving, he turned and said, "Oh, by the way, if the telephone rings, don't answer it."

Before getting into bed, I parted the window curtains, allowing the outside light to brighten the room for the Minister when he returned. I slept until 6 A.M., then left. The Minister was still asleep on the other bed.

Later that day, he asked how I had slept. I replied, "Fine, after I realized I could trust you."

"You think you were afraid!" he shot back. "I tossed and turned for hours, unable to sleep." Returning from the casino he had noticed the window curtains in his room were open. Suddenly the thought overwhelmed him that I was a spy, planted on him, a prominent black politician, to embarrass him publicly and ruin his career.

We talked some. He made one comment that we did not discuss. "You know, white women could destroy racism."

I repeated his comment to Linda Bernhardt, twenty-five years old, small and thin, with long dark hair.

"Yes, I accept that," Linda said. "I think at the root of racism— I'm not saying the root—is the white man's protection of his white woman: this has a lot to do with the putting down of the black man."

Linda is a young, white South African who detests apartheid. She attributes her attitudes to her childhood friendships with blacks, friendships developed and sustained through her own and her father's theatrical work. Linda manages and promotes black musicians and actors. She has more contact with educated, urban blacks than most white South African women her age.

Her house is in a row of small, old houses in Yeoville, a densely populated neighborhood. Her household is semicommunal. She grew up having servants, but now whoever lives in the house helps with cooking and cleaning.

Linda sat on the floor, her legs folded Buddha fashion.

I asked her to elaborate her point on relationships between white women and black men.

"When a white woman breaks away and makes contact with a black man, it has a different interpretation than that given a white man's contact with a black woman. This is especially true here," she said, "where people have such clearly defined roles. An independent woman is not acceptable. You do find cases where a white man genuinely falls in love with a black woman, but I think it's rare."

"What about the colored population?" I asked.

"The farmers who cross the border to have sex with black women in Lesotho and Swaziland are staunch Nationalists, German immigrants, policemen," Linda explained. "They don't think in terms of children or love but in terms of sex. Certainly, they are not having meaningful relationships.

"A lot of people don't understand the closeness that exists between black people—the informality, the openness. They don't understand black culture at all.

"You see a lot of white 'chicks' go out with the hip black 'guys' who are into jazz and disco; here the black woman is exploited, which is the usual case."

"Do you know white women in love with black men?" I asked.

"I was involved with a black man for about a year," Linda said. "It was a situation that nobody knew about because . . . you can't. It became very complicated because of the families and the society."

Linda could talk about this relationship; it was in the past. Now she has a white boyfriend, British.

"If you really care, you don't want the other person to be put in jail," Linda said. "No, it's not only the jail sentence, but the whole fear of exposure. The dirt of it. Like taking something that's pure and turning it into smut. It's very hard. Even a simple drive in a car becomes difficult."

She said it was easy to be involved with a black man for one night, but the terrible pressure made a permanent relationship impossible.

She talked about the difficulty—even paranoia—of just having black friends. At two o'clock one morning, some black musician friends drove to her house in Yeoville to drop off equipment. They left and she went back to bed. Suddenly she was startled by flashlights moving around her house.

"I looked through the window and saw police with spotlights.

Six or seven uniformed men walked up this way and into the back yard." She gestured toward the narrow alley between her house and the one next door. "They were wandering all through the garden. I heard somebody say, 'There are no kaffirs here,' but in Afrikaans.

"A woman in the apartment building across the street had called the police to say there were black people here. It was totally freaky.

"The worst thing about this country is that people, the man in the street, do the government's work. It doesn't matter if the person is black or white. The number of informers is in the thousands.

"You never know if who you're talking to is okay or not. This whole thing has turned brother against brother, best friends against each other in fear. Even in the townships you never know who or where or why.

"One of the most efficient outcomes of apartheid is how incredibly divided people are: Afrikaners keep to themselves; English keep to themselves. Then you have Jews, Italians, Rhodesians. Everybody keeps to themselves. In the black community you have divisions.

"Everyone is mistrustful. The Afrikaner mistrusts the English. The English mistrust one another. There's a hell of a lot of work to be done and it's got to be done by people together.

"In the sixties we used to have demonstrations and protest marches. Okay, those kinds of things are banned now. Today the problem is that you can't get enough people together to go on a protest march and immobilize the police. A hundred university students going on a march means nothing. If you got every northern suburban housewife to stand with the Black Sash that would mean something. But there are not enough people who are committed.

"Black Sash used to protest bannings and detentions. Yet throughout the history of the struggle it is only when the overseas press picks it up that it has any impact here.

"The repression is so effective it reaches into . . . for example, you're staying in a flat where your phone is tapped. Okay, you are not bothered. But I share a house with three people. The things I do affect them and we have to check it out with one another. They're very nervous about the phone being tapped.

"Take the people living in the suburbs, who might have their consciences pricked because so-and-so was detained. It's not a vast white community; so-and-so is a friend of so-and-so.

"Raymond Seton, who's serving eight or ten years for distributing pamphlets in Durban, grew up with me. We lived in the same building, his family and mine, for ten years. I never knew he was radical. We never had much to do with each other. The next thing, he's arrested in Durban. In that block of flats there were many people. It was a very friendly building. I wonder how those people reacted to Raymond's being sentenced for something like that and what effect it had on them."

"What do you think about the Progressive Federal Party?" I asked.

"People think the PFP is radical," Linda said. "But to me that party's coming into power would be diabolical. With the Nats you know exactly what you're facing. I've never been involved with young Progs because I've always thought it's bullshit. I don't believe in these cookery classes for domestic servants. Okay, literacy classes is a good idea, but it's not goddamn enough!

"We used to be a group of four. We went out and painted slogans on all the walls in town. 'Remember Sharpeville'—that kind of stuff. That's fine—but that was four of us. And to try to get more people now, you see . . .

"Basically, the whites are not prepared to share the country. They talk about superficial things: black people being allowed to go to the cinema or eat in the same restaurants."

"What do you see in the future?" I asked.

"We used to look at Mozambique and Angola and say, 'Twenty years.' But it took only five. That was a shock.

"As far as I'm concerned, things have really started to happen since 1975. Four years ago nobody would have said Rhodesia was anywhere near . . . The pace has increased tenfold."

"How long?" I asked.

"Maybe five years. I mean, I'm hoping. I don't believe twenty years. Maybe I'm naïve. But the spirit of black people has become stronger, more obvious.

"We used to be surrounded by white-ruled states. Those are all gone. There is only South Africa. It's touching us."

NO
CHOICE

Thenjie with Lumumba in Soweto the day she was released from Potchefstroom prison, where she had been held without charge

18

Detained

Woman

Three weeks after our visit to Thenjie in Potchefstroom prison, she was unexpectedly released after two and a half months in solitary. She talked nonstop on the drive back to Soweto.

An old woman neighbor, bent and gray-haired, tottered across the dirt yard through the open front door into the Mtintsos' small living room, which had quickly crammed with people. The old woman flung her stringy arms around Thenjie's narrow shoulders, moaning, "Why, why, why," tears brimming in her filmy eyes.

Despite her banning orders, Thenjie decided to make known the details to me of her first detention in August 1976. And for the next few weeks we met in the offices of the black Writers' Association of South Africa (WASA), the same offices occupied by the Black Consciousness groups before they were banned in 1977.

WASA national president Zwelakhe Sisulu made coffee for us— a rare act for a black man in South Africa. When he sloshed water in the Cremora jar to rinse the last of the powder into his cup, Thenjie laughed and said, "Boy! you really must have been poor when you grew up."

Zwelakhe worked for the black-run, white-owned newspaper, *The Post*. His father, Walter Sisulu, is one of the top ANC leaders imprisoned on Robben Island. His mother, banned for more than half of his twenty-seven years, was told in 1979 her banning order was extended for another two years.

Zwelakhe smiled at Thenjie's "poor" remark. He had once observed to me that it was surprising Thenjie had pulled herself from the poverty of her childhood to her leadership position. "The black community will continue to throw forward leaders such as her," he added.

Like other black journalists, Zwelakhe was forced to the forefront of the struggle after relating to the rest of the world what he saw in Soweto. Many journalists who had not believed in the Black Consciousness Movement were converted by the police killings or by their own detentions.

The WASA office was located in downtown Johannesburg. With the tape recorder between us, with the noise of traffic coming through the windows, with people taking voice lessons in an adjacent room, Thenjie related what happened to her during detention.

"They took me from my place to King William's Town police station, into the security offices. One security guy who was a boy . . . I can never forgive that boy—being assaulted by an eighteen-year-old Afrikaner, and a stupid boy at that. I really can't explain it. The physical pain was not so much. The pain was deep inside—that a stupid boy assaulted me. It was the pride that hurt. He beat me until I bled through my mouth.

"After that the seniors came and I reported the incident. They dismissed it and drove me to East London.

"There the security police wanted me to admit Steve Biko had organized boys to leave South Africa for military training, which I wouldn't.

"So, they made me stand in that room Thursday, Friday, Saturday, Sunday. I actually peed while standing there. They didn't allow me toilet, water, food—anything. I was just standing and they were changing shifts. Then the last day I sat down and said, 'Whoever wants me to stand will have to pick me up.'

"Which Steve had said was stupid. I should have done that right away. You see, Steve's attitude was he would never allow any man to beat or assault him or do anything to him without reacting. He used to say, 'These guys—the day they get me—they'll kill me, because I'll beat up the guy or make him beat me so that I just die. If my hands are tied, I will spit in his face. I'm not going to answer questions that I don't want to answer.' He asked me, 'Why did you stand? You could have just sat down and let them beat you.'

"When I went to jail, I thought I would do just that. We had discussed this. Don't let them beat you to a point where you think you can still save yourself by talking. Just make them angry so they beat you completely and next to death, when you can't spill the beans. If you allow yourself to be beaten just to a dangerous point, you're going to talk.

"But I stood. I can't justify standing. I still feel it was stupid. From the onset, I could have sat down and let them assault me. No, I stood those three days. And I had strength that was unbelievable. I don't know how I managed to do it. Today I can't stand for thirty minutes.

"After that, the beating continued—general assaulting. Then they left me for a week. By this time I had signed a statement, but the statement was my own. Parts of it were untrue but not dangerous to anybody. I alleged I knew Mapetla Mohapi had gone to Johannesburg. This was not true. I didn't know. But it could not affect Mohapi. He was dead. And it could not affect me. And I was just tired. So I said, yes, he had gone.

"After the week, they came every day and beat me. One thing they are good at: they can sit there for twelve hours and insult you. They. Can. Insult. You."

"What do they say?"

"How bitchy you are; they list the men you supposedly slept with. They insulted Steve, the work he did, the women he slept with.

"When you meet the security police, they adopt a certain stance: *kragdadig* (extremely tough), or polite gentlemen who pretend they don't want to beat you.

"Basically most of them are afraid. They are desperate. Whatever they do to you, they are doing out of fright. They feel they occupy a very important position because they can assure the electorate things are normal in this country. When you get into their clutches they want to destroy you.

"Did you see a doctor?"

"Not immediately. From the security offices I went to prison. I was under the General Law Amendment [which allows fourteen days without charge or access to lawyer and family]. They left me in the cell for seven days.

"Now this is the bad period. You don't know what they want. You don't know what they're going to do to you. You are anxious. You don't want to be afraid. But you're in detention and you're anxious. You have not adjusted. You don't know what to expect. And, remember, Mohapi had just died in the hands of these guys.

"They took me to an office, twelve of them in an empty office. One group was from Queenstown; they introduced themselves. There were some questions. I did not fool myself about answering. I would answer. They were stern guys. A stern Afrikaner is not very beautiful.

"I said, sure, I'll tell you everything you want. Which I did. They gave me paper and pen. I asked what do they want to know? They put down the questions. I answered all those questions honestly. They gave me the paper to take to my cell so I could write the statement there.

"I finished the statement in one day and handed it over. They said I must stick it up my ass. This was not the rubbish they wanted.

"And I said, 'Well, that's all I know.' Then interrogation started. They are animals. Their first question: 'We know you slept with Steve Biko, is that not so?'

" 'No.'

"They beat me and beat me, wanting me to say I slept with Steve Biko. They are animals. That's the problem. Then they named lots of men I'm supposed to have slept with. And I laughed, because I'm conservative about sleeping with men. It was a joke."

"Where did they beat you?"

"Just anywhere. It is called assault with intent. The first time this guy just claps [hits] me. A rather tough guy. I weighed about forty-six kilograms [101 pounds]. So when they clap you, they clap you. They punch you, you fall; they kick you; they lift you up.

"When interrogation became more serious, their assault was systematic. They made me stand next to the wall and the man next to me just hit my head on the wall like a ball, a tennis ball. N-kgoon, n-kgoon, n-kgoon. I had been wearing a beret. They removed it so bare head hit bare wall. At the end of three hours, my head, I could feel it growing.

"It was not really painful; funny, now that I think of it, I can't imagine the pain. But I was just going n-kgoon, n-kgoon, n-kgoon, n-kgoon. In fact, I was beginning to do it automatically.

"That is when they ask you particular questions. The thing they wanted most was my trips to Botswana. They couldn't imagine Thenjie traveling on an innocent journey to Botswana. I went there to see Geoff Baqwa. He owed us money and that was all. Obviously, I was not going to say, 'Baqwa, give me money,' and rush home. I had to know what people were doing and thinking.

"The danger was learning some of them had gone to Tanzania and Algeria for military training. And I didn't want to say that. I had a tight story which was true, that Baqwa left me in a house for exactly six hours. I didn't know anybody. I didn't know where we were. I was just in the house alone. Besides, I didn't have a lot of time to talk to Baqwa, so I didn't know what Baqwa was doing. That type of thing.

"Then they told me that my son Lumumba was dead. When they detained me in King William's Town, Lumumba was with me. They said the driver for the Zimele Trust Fund was driving my Volksy. They were chasing him. He was with Lumumba in the car. When you come through the Zanempilo clinic there's a ditch. The road sort of winds until you get to that ditch. And I could imagine, I could actually see them chasing him around those bends and he being forced off the road and, of course, going over the ditch. They showed me a photograph of a smashed Volkswagen. I didn't want to believe it, but I thought it could happen.

"So my stance was, okay, you have killed my child, let me go bury him. They wouldn't. I said, 'I'm not going to say anything from now on until I see that child or I bury him. You can kill me if you like, I'm not going to do anything.' I didn't. I just let them beat me, but I wouldn't talk. I wouldn't say one dirty word. Eventually, they showed up with Lumumba, after which I started answering questions.

"They left me for a few weeks. They came back one day, interrogated and beat me, and at five o'clock drove me to this place which I later identified as Kei Road, where Mohapi had died. They pushed me into this empty cell and said, 'This was Mohapi's cell. Perhaps he will tell you how he died. And he'll tell you that you must talk.' They read a statement that was supposed to be made by Mohapi incriminating Steve and myself. God knows. I didn't know what Mohapi was talking about. I had no idea. I found myself admitting some things that incriminated Mohapi. I said, 'Sorry, Mohapi, you are dead and buried.'

"They left me in this cell and came back with a big towel and a bucket of water. They immersed this towel in water, threw it over me, and tied it. What was bad was not the strangling, but the suffocation because this thing was wet. I could see how Mohapi had died. We hadn't been able to work out why Mohapi's head was thrown backwards. If he had hanged, his head would be down. But his head was back.

"This man was behind me. I was sitting on the floor between his thighs and he was strangling me. I kept trying to push him away. If he had overdone it, I could have died. He couldn't know how much I could take. I was weak; I had not had good food, exercise, you know.

"So I understood what happened with Mohapi: they did this, then realized the man was dead.

"With me, they did it, then left for some time. I would lie in a faint or be unconscious. They would revive me with water, do the same thing. They did it three times. On the third occasion, this guy actually asked, 'Now can you see how Mohapi died?'

"After that they took me back to the cell. There was a statement they wanted me to sign. I had not read the statement. The first page was fine: Thenjie born 1950, blah, blah, blah. But the second and third page I had not read so I refused. I can't sign a statement I have not read.

"So, ho, didn't they beat me! Now it was a different guy beating me, Van der Merwe, the head of the security police in the Eastern Cape. He's a very tough guy. You know, his clap just goes like this, the whole face. Oh, he beat me.

"Eventually they left me alone. I remained in my cell. For three weeks they did not come. Now this is their stance: They beat you and leave you alone and you sit there wondering what next. But it's not as bad as the first time when you don't know.

"One day I was sleeping and it was raining. They came and said I must take my clothes. They bundled me into a car and we drove toward Transkei. When we get to the Kei River it was raining cats and dogs. He showed me a car on the other side of the Kei River. That car was in the Transkei. I was in the Ciskei [tribal area] divided by the bridge.

"They said, 'See that car? Walk to that car.' It was raining. I had one problem—if I walked, they were going to shoot me in the back. They pushed me out of the car. I remained standing there for thirty minutes. I couldn't take the rain any longer. I decided to walk. Nothing happened. I was taken by the guys waiting in the Transkei car to a police station."

"Why did they do that? Why didn't they turn you over themselves?"

"They were just playing. I don't think they were even asked to do that. It was fun. They knew I was going to be frightened; they knew I was going to think about being shot; this was the fun of it.

"I was taken to a police station in Umtata (the major city of Transkei). In all of my experiences in jail, I have never felt so badly toward whites in general as I did when I went into that cell. In all my life, the assaults they inflicted on me were nothing compared to the pain I felt that day, which I can still feel today.

"That cell. It's a zinc cell. I can see it. There are two zinc buildings, corrugated iron. When the police opened this particular cell— apparently men had been sleeping in this one—you were welcomed by a stink which weighed heavily. You felt it not only with your nose; you felt it with your ears, your eyes, with every part of your body. You felt the smell. The cell had been cemented like a tarred road with potholes. The smooth part of the cement was completely gone.

"After they locked the cell, I could not find one corner which was not dirty. And the lice were moving. I could see them going up and down that wall. There was a bucket full of shit. It was green. There were these flies which were green and very big and made a sound when they moved. There were lots of them in that cell. I have never seen a cell as dirty as that. I have been in dirty cells, but that Umtata cell . . . And you know, it affected me. The blankets: jails have these gray blankets. These were not just dirty. I cannot describe them. You cannot imagine them unless you see them.

"I tried finding a corner to sit down. It was just a cell with that bucket and the blankets. I found a corner where the bucket had not done its turn. Apparently, the people who had been in the cell had moved the bucket from corner to corner, and it left its mark wherever it went. Eventually, I found a place and huddled there next to my pallet.

"When I looked at the blankets I could not imagine how I was going to sleep. I sat there and allowed myself to be angry. I'm not the crying type. I think I could have cried. But I just allowed my anger. I got angry. I got really angry. If a white man had marched into that cell I'm sure I would have hit him.

"I was not feeling logical, political—just emotional, angry. Later I sang one song, "Mabawuyeke." I cooled down and told myself, this is it. I am a freedom fighter. I cannot be depressed by a dirty cell and a full bucket.

"So. I settled down. I made the bed and I slept. The following day I had to clean the cell because I was told it was going to be my home. The alternative was to live in the cell as it was. The issue was the bucket which was green! People had been using that bucket for months and nobody emptied it. One alternative was to use the bucket too, like the others, and not empty it. But I couldn't. I still had to eat.

"It was raining outside. I had seen plates, dirty plates, broken plates, next to the cell. When I got into the cell I had seen a plate. The following day, the person who brought food took that plate as it was and put pap on it and gave it to me. A hunk of pap. Somebody had attempted cooking it, but had given up the idea. And I was supposed to eat that.

"The following day I asked for a broom. They didn't give it to me. Now, a police station is inconvenient. You can't even get thirty minutes' exercise in the morning or afternoon as you do in a prison. I remained in the cell for three solid days, bucket and all. They only opened it when they brought the chunk of food. Each day they fetch the chunk back and throw it away and bring a fresh one. And I was not eating.

"On the fourth day, a South African Police major came. I told him I wanted to clean the cell. He looked around. I could feel, I could see, he was embarrassed. He felt what I felt. He was black. But then, he was a policeman. He couldn't do anything. He was supposed to keep me there.

"But, later, they brought a broom and a bucket for water. And, of course, I had to go empty the bucket and wash it.

"I have been dehumanized in my life. But that is one experience which urges me on whenever I think of the things we have to go through because of this system.

"It was raining the day I carried the bucket on my head. It was heavy; it was full. We couldn't use the drain which was in the yard. We had to use a drain in the main street in Umtata. So I carried it, emptied it, went to wash it. No amount of washing . . . I was using my hands, my bare hands . . .

"But I cannot describe the lice that were there. They were as big as this. I don't know how I managed to sleep each night because those lice, they went to town on me. As luck would have it, there were bees, too. And it was hot, hot. I had to lie under blankets during the day because the bees were loose. I complained but there were only three cells.

"Then these guys come to fetch me in the second week. They beat me, but not as badly as in East London."

"Have you ever been beaten by blacks?"

"No. By whites. Except one time in Soweto, when black police were herding demonstrators into vans.

"But in Umtata it was just general assault. That's also where they hung me. You know when we hang clothing on a hanger? The hanger hooks on that rod? I was hooked like the hanger."

"You mean they tied you there?"

"Yes. The issue was still the statement. I was supposed to sign it.

"Then something very beautiful happened. I was coming out of the security office and a cousin of mine saw me. We had never met. But he had seen my pictures in The Daily Dispatch. I didn't know him at all. So I passed and he stared at me. I smiled. It was automatic. When you are a prisoner, you want people to recognize you. So I smiled and he left.

"He came to the police station. The police told him who I was. The Transkei police didn't know the Terrorism Act; they allowed him into my cell.

"They allowed him to bring food. I had not been eating, only bread on some days. Even before that, something happened to brighten my days. Ralph's [Lumumba's father] sister saw me as I was brought out of the building. She followed us, found me, and gave me some money.

"The wardress was a little thirteen-year-old uneducated girl. She earned 2.50 rands a month. I gave her 1 rand a week to bring me bread and milk and some papers. She didn't know she wasn't allowed. I didn't tell her. I let her buy *True* magazine and *Hair*. There was nothing more beautiful than fooling the police. While they beat you, you smile and think: He doesn't know I'll be reading *Hair* magazine tonight. It's very little but you rush into your cell and read and feel on top of the world. You eat that dry bread with milk. And you laugh at the idea.

"My cousin brought me lunch—curry and things—and gave me money. I got the girl to buy me hamburgers, fish and chips. Under my pallet, I kept lots of novels and *The Daily Dispatch*. Sometimes she would plait my hair and I'd plait hers.

"Then one day the security police were parked behind my cell. They saw my cousin bring food. They opened the door. I couldn't hide the plate. There was no place but the bucket. So they said, 'Huh, is that so!' I didn't feel bad at all. You can never defeat prisoners. They moved me to another prison.

"Ngqamakwe was not bad. They were not beating me. Sunset was the end of the day; no electricity; you just slept.

"Then I was transferred to Nqanduli. There I discovered a friend. The wardress and I were in school together. She sent food and, of course, the police found out. I was chucked out.

"In Lebode there were two cells, mine and the other with about four prisoners. I used to hear them talk. We shared a common yard. They used to say: 'She's said to have killed a person; that's why she is here.' All kinds of speculating. They thought I couldn't understand Xhosa. So I said, 'No, man, just listen why.' They said, 'Oh, shame.'

"I was there for three weeks.

"Then out of the blue, they came. The security. I had not seen them for a month. They took me back to Umtata and who did I see there but my mother and Lumumba. My mother's story was that somebody saw me carrying a bucket in the center of town and told Father Stubbs (Anglican priest, friend of Biko and of Thenjie). He put my mother on a plane to Umtata. She went from police station to police station, prison to prison, and said, 'I'm not moving until you produce her.'

"So they produced me. We talked for thirty minutes. My mother told me she was returning home with Lumumba. I returned to security headquarters and they tell me they are releasing me on condition that I get on a bus and out of the Transkei immediately.

"I thought my mother was catching that very bus. But she decided to leave the following morning. So I got into the bus. I couldn't get off because I didn't have a passport. They had told the driver. I asked if the bus would stop before it got to East London. I had a feeling there was a trick somewhere.

"We stopped in East London. There were the security police. I was redetained and whisked to King William's Town, where I joined Ramphele Mamphela, Thoko Mpumlwana, Phumla Sangotsha, Nobandile Mvovo. They had been there since August.

"So I talked for . . . they were tired . . . I was talking. Mamphela said, 'Hooooo, God, aren't you going to sleep? When is she going to stop?' I hadn't seen anybody, and I had something to talk about.

"I was there for a month. They came to ask if my car was in order. I said, 'How can I know? I have been in jail.' That's when they bundled me into their car and accompanied me to Ginsburg to fetch a suitcase, so I could not talk to anyone.

"Now the beauty of the police: They can dramatize things. They put me into a police van from King William's Town. One van, one set of security. From Queenstown to Aliwal North, another set, another car. From Aliwal North to Bloemfontein, another set and another car.

"Bloemfontein, I was locked up in a cell, slept there. Eight A.M., another car to Kroonstad. Kroonstad, another car to Vereeniging. Vereeniging to John Vorster Square. Then from John Vorster to Orlando" (in Soweto, where she was restricted to her mother's home until December 12, 1981).

Thenjie's banning orders require her to report to the police station in Soweto the first Monday of every month. In addition she cannot go into colored or Asian areas; she cannot visit factories, publishing houses, educational institutions; she cannot attend the trials of others or political, social, and educational gatherings. She can speak with one person at a time, but not with another banned person.

However, in the black community those who are banned receive emotional support and are recognized as the true leaders, in contrast to government-approved black officials.

When security police arrive, now and then, to check out Thenjie's home for illegal materials, she bundles banned books around her mother's body, under the voluminous dress, before opening the door. Mrs. Mtintso walks slowly, replying noncommittally to police inquiries.

Despite restrictions, Thenjie continues to travel on the premise that "to them all blacks look alike." She meets with friends in her Soweto home while listening for police cars, ready to dart if necessary.

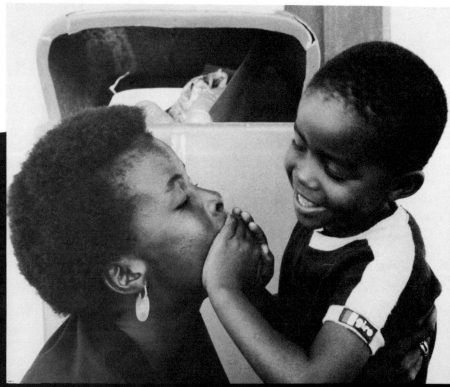
Thenjie and Lumumba in Lesotho

19

No Good-byes

At 8:30 P.M., January 15, 1979, my phone rang.

"I'm in trouble," Thenjie said. The connection was cut. Were police trying to detain her for a sixth time?

In a few minutes, the phone rang again.

"The police came to my house today while I was at work, and again this evening." Thenjie continued as if she had not been interrupted. "They are coming at 6:30 A.M. tomorrow to take me to court. But courts don't open until 9 A.M., and magistrates, not security police, are the ones who order people to appear in court."

She told the police she would drive to court in her own car, and not be taken by police.

The next morning I met her at the sprawling old rock courthouse on Fox Street. At 9 A.M. Thenjie reported to the court officials. She must appear in the courtroom in one hour to be charged with breaking her banning order. She had traveled illegally—as she had done so often—but this time, several months previously, she had been caught stepping off an airplane north of Pretoria.

While we awaited the appointment with the judge, Thenjie and another banned black person conversed on the steps of the courthouse, across from the Anglo-American mining conglomerate and a few blocks from the Johannesburg Stock Exchange. Descending the courthouse steps, the black man waved to Thenjie. The two shouted in English across the wide steps. Afterward, she said, "He's banned. He's afraid. That's why he did not come closer."

One hour later, Thenjie entered the cramped wood-paneled room. The clerk summoned "Ethel Thenjiwe Mtintso." She strode forward, her head high, and stood in the center of the room. The magistrate read her charge and remanded her to trial on February 16, one month from that day. The authorities held hard proof that she had violated her banning order. They could imprison her for several years.

On January 22, near a garage repairing her car, Thenjie said, "I hope you can keep a secret. I'm leaving tomorrow morning. I had planned to go last night, but friends came to my house. I prepared supper for them and they stayed late. This morning I could not bear to leave them."

Thenjie pulled away in the VW, gazing straight ahead through large sunglasses. I wondered how this woman, well known to the police, driving a yellow car, and accompanied by a five-year-old child, could escape.

During the next week I waited. Tuesday, Wednesday, Thursday—seven days. Then there was a phone call from Soweto.

"Thenjie and Lumumba are safe in Lesotho." Between 1976 and 1979, more than four hundred black political activists had fled through Lesotho, a black-ruled country in the midst of white-ruled South Africa.

On February 2, Thenjie's escape was headlined in the black edition of *The Rand Daily Mail*. The paper also recorded that security police appeared at Thenjie's Orlando home on February 1 to take her mother to a police station for an hour's questioning. Where was Thenjie? police wanted to know. Did the family have relatives in neighboring countries?

Reactions among Thenjie's friends were surprise and dismay. Reebs Musi was shocked. She had no idea Thenjie would leave. She felt cut adrift.

Kitty Duma and I visited Mrs. Mtintso. I expected her to be sad, but Kitty predicted: "Any mother would be happy to know her child was safe, even if she couldn't see her again."

The gray-rimmed pupils of Hannah Mtintso's eyes did not conceal their gleam.

As she touched the top of her expansive bosom, she said, "Inside I was always worrying when Thenjie didn't come home. I'm very happy. Thenjie's father was Congress (ANC), and then Thenjie. I don't know where she gets it. I'm not brave," Mrs. Mtintso laughed.

Several days later Thenjie phoned me from Maseru, the capital of Lesotho, asking me to "Please, when you come, bring my box of earrings from my mother's house."

A couple of weeks later I delivered the earrings and money from Zwelakhe Sisulu for linoleum for the cement floor of a room Thenjie had found to stay in.

As we talked, casino machines clashed and clanked behind us in the Holiday Inn where I was booked. Thenjie glanced around the lobby. "Our people have been kidnapped from here, from this very place," she said. "Lesotho is infiltrated with South African police." She pulled Lumumba closer to her.

Thenjie described her escape, leaving out details which might endanger others who would take the same route.

She had left in the morning while it was still dark. She had stopped after two hours, parked the car, and taken a nap. When she awoke she was tempted to turn back to Soweto. "It really struck me what exile, what leaving home, meant."

The gravel road she took was mountainous with winding turns, and sometimes it disappeared. "I was afraid I'd just disappear, and nobody would know. If you miss a particular turn, you'll go right down."

"I was more concerned about Lumumba and began to think I should have left him at home. At one point when the road was bad, Lumumba said, 'Let's not go to this Maseru. I know you are afraid of police, but let's go back.'

"I said, 'No, I'm not afraid of police, Mumbas.' It hurt me that he could not understand. I could only say, 'You see, I get detained frequently and I'm not with you all this time, so I want to be with you always.' He said, 'I'm going to miss my granny. You should have taken her along too; then we'd all be together.'

The pain of exile had begun. But her friend, Father Stubbs, who was in Lesotho, remarked: "Thenjie is open to whatever happens. I can no more say what direction she will go than I can predict how things in general will go. All I can say is, unless she's physically destroyed, she will be there at . . ."

His sentence faded. The final word was understood: "liberation."

Thenjie in Lesotho

20

Survivalist

A year later, I was in New York finishing work on this book when I received a phone call from Thenjie in Lesotho. After relating her latest, futile attempt to secure a visa, which would allow her to reenter Lesotho after travel in other countries, she said, "I've switched organizations." Neither she nor I were about to state names over the phone. We didn't have to; I understood. She had called because she wasn't sure how, or if, this development would affect information in the book.

I said I would like to talk with her and would try to be in Lesotho by the end of the month.

"I'll be here," she replied and hung up.

Thenjie's "switch" meant she had left the Black Consciousness organization, whose policies had so fired her and for which she had been tortured; it meant she had aligned herself with the African National Congress (ANC) and with armed struggle. What would Steve Biko have said?—a question she must have asked herself many times. Had she found an answer that satisfied her emotionally as well as politically?

I remembered what Thenjie's friend, Reebs Musi, had said. "After Steve's death, things didn't really come to a stop. We always felt at some stage or other one of us is going to die and it doesn't mean the end of the world. There is this belief among black people that when one dies, he lives with you spiritually, a sort of god with a small 'g.' Those who are dead know and see whatever you do."

She paused, then added, "Wherever Steve is, he wouldn't be happy if we stopped. He would be happy to see us going on and on and on."

I phoned the Lesotho mission at the United Nations and was told as an American I did not need a visa if I went as a tourist. The

South African government denied my request for a visa but gave no reason.

On the first leg of my journey toward Maseru, the capital of Lesotho, I thought about Thenjie's political decision and it seemed inevitable, given the context of the war in South Africa. Yet even a year ago, the choice had not been self-evident. But now there appeared a semblance of order, an identifiable process.

Thenjie's decision to join ANC could not be isolated from the life-and-death struggle for power in South Africa. Her choice was a significant indication of the path other young revolutionaries would follow.

But what ingredients had gone into making that choice? I was on my way to find out.

In London, I boarded the British Airways plane to Johannesburg. In the next seat, a black man from the Luo tribe in Kenya, noticing the South Africans sitting around us, commented, "I looked at them when I first got on and said to myself, these are different whites." He smiled. He was serious. Dressed in an expensive suit, he was returning from an international monetary conference in London. He slept with the purple airlines blanket stretched over his head, glad to deplane in Nairobi.

Circling Soweto at midday, we could see the coal smoke swirling upward near the gold-mine slag heaps.

At Jan Smuts Airport in Johannesburg I boarded the two-propeller Air Lesotho plane for Maseru. We flew over the magnificent flat farms of the Orange Free State and then up and around the beveled mountains of Maseru, one here, another there— the beauty, breathtaking.

Lesotho, a small, black-ruled country granted independence from Britain in 1966, is completely surrounded by white-ruled South Africa and is self-sufficient only in eggs and blankets. An eight-hour drive from Johannesburg, the tiny mountainous land is recognized internationally as an independent African country. Yet its economy is closer to that of a homeland for the Sotho tribe. Able-bodied men are forced to leave wives and children in rural poverty to seek work in the mines of South Africa.

Refugees arriving here from the highly industrialized areas of Johannesburg are taken aback by the cows and sheep that roam the streets, the Basotho people wearing blankets during the hottest weather, the mere five or six traffic lights in downtown Maseru. The refugees adjust to these differences. The greater disappointment is the lack of freedom in this independent country. It is infiltrated by South African agents. Political activity is nearly as hazardous as in South Africa. ANC men have been detained by the Lesotho security police for long periods of time. In 1979, a black nationalist had his arm badly burned by a letter bomb.

Arriving in Lesotho, I left a message for Thenjie at a particular shop, then checked into the Victoria Hotel. Outside my window a mountain hung like a backdrop—like a local mohair rug patterned with simply drawn houses, sheep, and a zigzag road. I watched a girl walking, straightened by the baby strapped to her back; an old man, flashing his cane back and forth, stopping to pee.

At sunset, the mellow light drew inky, long shadows. There seemed nothing beyond the mountain.

All afternoon I had listened to the South African news on the radio. Three black men were holding twenty-five white hostages in a bank in Silverton, a suburb of Pretoria. The men considered themselves on an urban guerrilla mission. The reporter identified them as terrorists on a suicide mission. The men held the hostages seven hours, then police stormed the bank, killing the three black men and two of the white hostages.

When Thenjie arrived at my hotel, we began to talk as usual without preliminaries, but also as though a year had not passed. Her hair was plaited in an intricate pattern and silver earrings dangled from her ears.

Thenjie, who had never before traveled outside of South Africa, described her initial response to an exile's life in Lesotho.

"Day dawns, sun sets, there's nothing. At home in Orlando, I used to lie in my bed and look back at what I had accomplished that day. But the exile syndrome sets in: nothingness. Even at Black Consciousness meetings, we just talked round and round, our discussions not seriously directed at the enemy."

When she first arrived, her friends already there from King William's Town invited her to stay with them. Later, she too would provide a transit house for new refugees. At the house of Silumki Sokupa (Soks), former Black Consciousness leader, the poverty of exile was stark. Soks, his pregnant wife, and their child slept on sponge mattresses and ate sitting on the floor because there was no table.

"The house was just cemented—no ceiling, no electricity."

Each refugee receives 30 rands ($34.50) a month from the United Nations Commission for Refugees. In Soweto, Thenjie could hardly make ends meet on 300 rands a month.

"The people here get a bit wild when they hear your language," she said. "You speak Xhosa; they speak Sesotho. The Basothos don't like refugees much."

She described her present living arrangements as a "loose commune; others have tighter communes than ours."

She lives in a three-room brick house with cement floors. A wooden outhouse is hidden by weeds and tall grass in a fenced-in front yard. ANC pays the 40-rand-a-month rent, provides gas for the car, and basic food staples. Thenjie and her roommates use their 30 rands for whatever else they need.

In the tradition of African women, she cooked for her male roommates. Recently, however, she realized the unfairness of the tradition and has on occasion insisted the men cook for themselves.

Without my asking, she explained that Lumumba was back in Soweto with his grandmother. Her decision to part with him before Christmas had been wrenching. For five years she had kept him at her side. "I'm proud of the way I coped without help from anyone. But when my money ran out, I realized an exile's life was too hard for a little boy.

"When Lumumba got back to his granny he complained he couldn't have any ice cream in Lesotho; and there was no pull to flush the toilet." Her house is without running water; the outhouse is a pit toilet. Since she left Soweto, several people have moved in with her mother in the tradition of the extended family, which Lumumba has joined.

"I think of my child and I become even more determined to fight," she said. "He too will experience things which will motivate him to fight later on.

"I was ten during Sharpeville. I saw people struck by guns. I remember running with the crowd, singing 'Let Africa Return,' giving the ANC sign; that's how Lumumba will remember 1976 in Soweto. He already knows the *amandla* sign and what apartheid is."

I told her that friends in London had inferred she was joining ANC for "sentimental reasons," to be with and marry Lumumba's father, Ralph Mgijima.

She said Ralph had flown to Lesotho to see her. She had demurred about marriage, but warned if he later heard she had joined ANC, not to think it was because of him.

"No," she said, "not for sentimental reasons." Her decision to join was made for "deeply felt political reasons," the details of which she would outline later.

But that first day we discussed little in depth. It was pay day, the one day a month when refugees flooded Maseru to collect 30 rands at the Ministry of the Interior. Thenjie left to wait on line with the others.

The next day we met at her house. Given the sparse furnishings inside, the auburn, wood-carved entrance was incongruously elegant. When the sun set, orange stripes crossed the back window, while a fat moon loomed outside the front door.

In the kitchen were two small tables, a gas-run Primus stove, a tall enameled cabinet, and several large plastic buckets of water, which are filled at the public tap a mile away. Providing electricity by stretching wires from a nearby pole would cost 600 rands ($690). The house is lit by a kerosene lamp and candles.

Thenjie explained she had not gone into exile just to escape a sixth detention, but had departed on a multipronged mission assigned her by the Black Consciousness leadership.

She was to do a survey on refugees, for which she received a salary for six months from the Geneva-based World University Services. Black Consciousness leaders were interested in developing communal agricultural plans and setting up a Steve Biko educational institute. But above all else, they wanted her to explore the possibility of unifying the two black liberation movements: ANC and the Pan African Congress (PAC), which had splintered off from ANC in the late fifties.

One factor that divides the two black nationalist organizations is the Sino-Soviet split, which has affected leftist movements around the world. ANC, through association with the South African Communist Party, is purportedly aligned with Moscow, and PAC with Peking.

Both organizations compete for each new refugee who flees South Africa. The official South African estimate is that about five thousand people fled into neighboring nations during and after "Soweto." Of these it is estimated that two thousand have undergone military training. Although figures could not be proved, the ANC claimed in 1980, at the height of the exodus, that it had the allegiance of 70 percent of Lesotho's several hundred refugees. Other reports say more than 12,000 people fled South Africa in the mid- and late 1970s, and three-fourths of them joined the ANC.

New recruits receive military training in Africa and, occasionally, in Eastern Europe before reentering South Africa to join the urban guerrilla underground. No one, not even wives and husbands, know where they are—unless they are captured or killed.

Although in no way pressured by ANC to join, Thenjie later discovered a top ANC leader had written to ask about her politics.

Her reputation, word of her abilities and potential had preceded her arrival.

When she did arrive, no viable Black Consciousness organization existed. She set about organizing the few refugees who had not joined ANC or PAC. "I felt lonely—not socially, but politically. I didn't know how to explain my assignment to friends in ANC without having them cluck over the way Black Consciousness wasted its money. They were bad months for me," she said.

However, in February and March, Michael (Baba) Jordan, a Black Consciousness man, and Tami Zani, publicity secretary for the Black Consciousness organization the Black People's Convention, fled to Lesotho. Zani took over as leader of the small group around Thenjie, who could relax for the first time. "Only then did I realize how tense I had been."

She did not mention the arthritis pain she endured throughout Lesotho's cold winter, and which was intensified by the cement floor in the house. This information was shared by Baba Jordan, who said, "I felt so sorry; she was in such agony because of the arthritis in her leg; we had to carry her to the hospital."

After six months, her survey grant expired. She tried to find work to sustain herself and Lumumba, who was still with her, but was unsuccessful. She described one job she did not get. The government had opened a new primary school in a remote, poverty-stricken mountain area. No one else applied for the teaching post, which paid 70 rands ($80.50). Nevertheless, she was rejected because she did not have a teaching certificate. Many teachers in the country had less education than she. The school had been near the Masiti mission, where her old friend Father Stubbs lived.

Thenjie told Father Stubbs about joining ANC. At first he too thought it was because she intended to marry Ralph. "Sometimes I just let people think what they want. But he was surprised because he knows how I hate violence. I can't take revenge; you can do anything to me and I become angry but, when it's all calm again, I cannot hit you for what you have done."

She told Father Stubbs she didn't like the feeling in Christianity of someone peering over her shoulder; it made her feel guilty. Her idea of God was of a protector. "In fact, I transform him into a human being."

"Are you in the process now of working out what you think about Christianity?" I asked.

"I'm not going to work it out; it's not an important aspect of my life."

"You used to think it was," I said.

"I made it important. It was a state of mind.

"Even when I did talk about Christianity, I was holding onto a supernatural power that exists after the ego ends, which you cannot control, and which cannot give you any answers.

"When Father Stubbs talks about Christianity, I tend to go off; my mind doesn't grasp it all. When he explains why he thought Steve Biko was a Christian, I can accept it, that Steve was not a Christian, but unintentionally, he became Christ, the savior of our people. He fought for the kind of justice Christ stood for. He died the way Christ died, that we may live. Now Steve has joined—how to call it—the holy spirits, let's say; and while his own spirit lives in us, we pursue what Steve stood for.

"But on the whole I'm fed up with Christianity. In South Africa, it's used to perpetuate slavery. Most youth rebel against Christianity. They see how its philosophy of turning the other cheek allows the white rulers to control black minds. Looking to Christ for salvation, you don't do anything on your own."

She described how the South African whites extract segments of the Bible to secure black acquiescence. "For example, in chapter 13 of Hebrews in the New Testament, Paul says, 'Obey them that have the rule over you, and submit yourself.' It just helps the Vorsters stay in authority; one must follow the authority," Thenjie said. "Blacks get hit every day and then some say, 'Oh, it's God's will.'

"Christians say they don't fight for material things in this world, but fight for the hereafter. So the oppression in this world is not their problem. Whites have instilled this in blacks."

"But whites do fight for possessions."

"Exactly. Exactly," she said. "The whites are not as Christian as we are. When I was in jail, I said, 'Oh, God is providing.' It was an escape. Father Stubbs said it was not an escape, that God was revealed to me. Even now I'm not an atheist. I don't dismiss him. Just in case he's there, I'm not going to denounce him."

I laughed and said, "That's practical." However, Thenjie had been very serious. She had not sat down to analyze Christianity, "only the South African blend and its weaknesses. The work of the missionaries leaves much to be desired."

During our next discussion in my hotel room, Thenjie made use of the electricity, ironing her own and her roommates' clothing and sheets on a towel spread on the floor.

Thenjie was convinced now there was no way for blacks to win power in South Africa without armed struggle. She said it had taken her so long to reach this understanding because of an "almost fanatic need to push the peace."

To give our discussion a more historical than individual context, she traced the black struggle from 1652, when Africans were first displaced from their land and cattle, to 1912, when ANC was founded.

She pointed out that for fifty years ANC conducted only peaceful protests: for example, the Defiance Campaign, in which blacks sat on "whites-only" benches, or their demonstrations against the pass laws.

When the response to these nonviolent activities was gunfire, with death and detention—and not change—as the consequence, Africans were forced to make a painful decision. They abandoned civil disobedience for guerrilla tactics. And in 1961, after Sharpeville, ANC formed Umkonto we Sizwe (Spear of the Nation); and PAC launched its military wing, Poqo (Go It Alone).

"Then from 1968 to 1977," she said, "it was the era of Black Consciousness, different from the ANC/PAC era in two specific ways. First, Black Consciousness addressed the colonized mentality of the oppressed and worked to overturn it. Secondly, we spoke only to black people and ignored the whites.

"In Soweto, 1976, the kids demonstrated peacefully against Afrikaans, and you know what happened. Kids were dying and I was watching. Those kids were making shields out of dust-bin lids to use against guns—kids who were ten, fifteen, twenty years old. The government statistics didn't reveal half the number of people who died.

"After Soweto, after Mapetla Mohapi was killed, after Biko was killed, after my last detention, my belief in a nonviolent victory lost all validity.

"It dawned on me when I was traveling from King William's Town to Johannesburg, being shifted from one car to another like a prisoner of war, every white policeman treating me as though I'd murdered a hundred people, when I had never even directed my anger against whites, only against myself and the black man . . . then I realized the need for armed struggle. Of course, when they killed Steve . . . that to me was final."

It never had occurred to Thenjie to leave the country for military training. Instead, she saw herself inside South Africa preparing others to support, assist, and protect the guerrillas.

When she fled to Lesotho, although convinced blacks should take up arms, she was still in accord with the Black Consciousness objective in exile: to fight under a United Patriotic Front. The reason it seemed possible to forge unity between ANC and PAC was that both organizations needed new blood; if Black Consciousness members denied this new blood, the two exiled movements could be persuaded to unite.

"That was the theory," Thenjie said. "In practice the strategy was futile.

"ANC and PAC wouldn't even talk about merging to Black Consciousness people, let alone to each other. When you said to a PAC person, 'Let's go talk with ANC,' he replied, 'With those communists?' And the ANC person said, 'What? Talk with those capitalists? Those racists? No, man, you must be out of your mind.'

"The irony was that ANC and PAC were putting the squeeze on Black Consciousness; they were determined not to allow a third liberation movement."

"What do you mean by the squeeze?" I asked.

"The African states in the Organization of African Unity refused to recognize Black Consciousness outside South Africa. Then, money from sponsors was cut off."

Although no longer with Black Consciousness, she continues to support it. "Black Consciousness has its limitations; it liberates people psychologically but not physically. Nevertheless, it is a process on the way to armed struggle. Inside South Africa, Black Consciousness is still necessary above ground; while ANC works underground. The two should function separately."

Recently she had learned about the ANC people inside South Africa and was amazed and impressed by the way they functioned throughout the society. By then she had begun to study the history of ANC and PAC. She had criticisms of both organizations, but her most severe judgment came down on PAC. The exclusivity of the Black Consciousness Movement had led many, herself included, to think its philosophy was an outgrowth of PAC. The name Azania, adopted in 1975 by Black Consciousness, was derived from PAC.

"My understanding was superficial, but even before I left home I began to see the limitations of PAC's Africanism. When we talked of Africanism in Black Consciousness, it was not an end, as it is with PAC, but the means to rid the black of his inferiority complex. I knew that we would open our doors to whites eventually. We were fighting for a nonracist society.

"In particular, PAC members dislike the statement in ANC's 1955 Freedom Charter: 'South Africa belongs to all who live in it, black and white.' PAC is suffering from internal leadership problems, a lack of programs and direction . . . also, its alliances."

"What alliances?" I asked.

"China. I'm moving away from China, which is veering toward

America. Western investment continues to support the South African system. But PAC is still moving with China.

"I realize PAC has only been in existence a relatively short time; perhaps not long enough to have a developed policy, which is also hampered by their leadership struggles.

"But one thing I cannot forgive is PAC fighting side by side with the South African Defense Force (1975) against a progressive force like MPLA [the Angolan liberation movement which won the struggle for independence from Portugal]. This cannot be excused as an error or seen as a PAC blunder; it showed where their politics were."

Thenjie said she had "hang-ups" about ANC, too, that it might be controlled by communists, especially white communists. "While I agree with the alliance between ANC and the South African Communist Party, I don't think a liberation movement should be controlled by the Communist Party.

"Some people criticize ANC for its diffuse absorption of people," she said, "from Christians and capitalists to Marxists. One woman said ANC is like an omnibus which stops at every bus stop and takes on all sorts of people, so you can't be sure who you are with. As a mass movement ANC must cater to everyone. It has basic principles but no strict ideology. You cannot say it is Marxist because there are people in ANC who are not Marxist."

"Do you think there will be socialism after liberation?" I asked.

"There's no guarantee, but there is dual membership: people can belong to both ANC and the Communist Party. Also, the Communist Party ideology does feed ANC somewhat. There are many black communists in ANC who are working to make sure capitalism will be abolished."

Thenjie believes the goal of the revolution is two-pronged: to address the issue of race, which she calls nationalism, and to dismantle a capitalist economy. "In South Africa, a rural person understands mainly racial oppression and not any class analysis. People will mobilize first around nationalism. Black Consciousness deals very well with the national question; its ideology of black pride cannot be banned.

"White racism exists . . . it is there . . . and the rulers use it to perpetuate capitalism. So I cannot see only a race solution in South Africa, without building a socialist economy as well.

"ANC's program is far from socialist," she said, "but most blacks who are socialists are members of ANC."

"Are you a socialist?" I asked.

"I feel I am, but socialism means so many things to so many people. Just saying one is is not enough. I have to find out more about it. But capitalism—thank you." She swished her hands across each other in a clap of dismissal.

"What about communism?" I asked.

"I've not studied it sufficiently, but I think I could become a communist. There was a stage at home when one revolted against communism; it was depicted as some kind of animal. At another stage, one fell in love with communism because it was so feared by the status quo it had to be something good. I've got to see what this communism is about. That's why I'm keen on traveling."

While I was in Lesotho, Thenjie made a dramatic discovery and arrived at my hotel room excited.

"I just learned my father was in the Communist Party," she said. "This morning I was reading this book and suddenly I was reading his name, Guna Makabeni. He was on the central committee of the South African Communist Party.

"The book (*Fifty Fighting Years: The Communist Party of South Africa, 1921–1971*, by A. Lerumo) mentions Guna Makabeni three times. In 1929, he campaigned for S. P. Bunting, a white communist who ran for a seat in parliament but lost."

Thenjie repeated the book's description of her father: "His reasoned and militant appeal to the rural African voters made a deep impression."

She had known her father was active in labor-union organizing and also had trained workers to use tractors.

"Now I see my working-class background," she said. "Now I see I was not just a delinquent. I see how I've reached this point. It's something I don't regret. In fact, I'm happy. Unless I understood suffering first hand, I'd be involved out of sympathy. But I know hunger. I know having no money in the house. My whole being has been one of need, all sorts of need. Even love. I've needed love, but my mother had no time to give it; she woke up early, left for work, and came home tired. How could I be anything but a freedom fighter?

"You take all the Soweto students from the representative councils, boys now in detention on Robben Island; they come from the urban working class. While they were in jail, I used to visit their homes and was moved by their parents—simple people who didn't understand what it was all about. But all of them supported their kids. The Silverton boys killed in the bank . . . their parents called them soldiers."

The Soweto burial of the three black men killed in the Silverton bank precipitated a demonstration. Crowds of black people swayed through Soweto streets to mourn the young men; they carried signs reading: "They were not terrorists; they are heroes." Except for the black-run *Post* and weekly *Voice,* all newspapers referred to the young men as terrorists. The liberal *Rand Daily Mail* made a policy decision to describe such men in the future as terrorists. When, the same month, caches of Russian-made weapons were reportedly discovered in Natal, white paranoia and fear escalated. Hundreds of whites joined suburban units of the "civil defense force."

"The Silverton men knew they risked death," Thenjie said. "A type of death I would accept for myself. I must not live—God help me—in exile until I'm eighty, fighting in theory. If we don't get back our country in the next few years, I must return and fight. I wouldn't like to sit here in 1990 and see we are still at it."

Suddenly, Thenjie said, "If I had my way, I'd go for military training before anything else. That's how I feel. But, then, ANC has its programs and fits people in accordingly.

"I mean, without training, how would I carry out a guerrilla mission? Let's say, hypothetically, I'm supposed to throw a grenade at someone's house, but I know he's with his kids. If I wasn't trained, I would not be able to do it. Or, say I'm just about to throw a grenade and an innocent little baby comes out; I would think, 'Oh, shame, a two-year-old.' It would be spontaneous to look at the child and say I can't destroy."

To Thenjie, the goal of a guerrilla war in South Africa is "to bring the rulers to the negotiating table as it did in Zimbabwe.

"If I am sent into South Africa on a mission, even if I die there, I would have lived, fought, and died for my beliefs. I would be satisfied."

"But how could you endure training—with your leg? Wouldn't the arthritis make it impossible?" I asked.

"I think I can overcome that," she replied. "Depends on the type of training. But I would take the training; if I discovered I couldn't make it physically, I would know I had tried.

"I spent months learning to walk." She was referring to the YWCA etiquette class in Soweto. "According to them, I will never walk properly—like a lady. Well, I've done things without a ladylike walk. I can still use my feet to get from one point to another."

On Sunday, we went to the cinema together—both our going together and the fact a cinema was open on Sunday would have been illegal in neighboring South Africa. The film was about the Vietnam war. In it, a soldier had a bad leg, which he dragged when he walked. Thenjie whispered, "If he can do it, so can I."

Afterward, we drove to the Holiday Inn for a lamb-chop lunch. I looked out the dining-room window at the mammoth furrowed field stretching beyond a muddy river; a mile or so away nestled a collection of small houses, a black township.

Thenjie, following my gaze, said softly, "That's my country . . . there . . . across the Caledon river."

"That's South Africa?" I said, "so close?"

She nodded.

A few days later at the airport, I waited for Thenjie, who was coming to see me off.

The discussions of the past weeks had revealed a woman more vulnerable than before. A woman faced with her own lack of knowledge about the world outside. She craved more education, yet refused to attend school unless it would further her political goals. She yearned to travel and see, firsthand, all of Africa, particularly socialist countries. She had moved from being a top-rank member of the Black Consciousness Movement to being a recruit on the bottom rung of the ANC ladder.

"I had no choice" and "I am a survivalist" were two of her recurring statements.

She had also made clear that for black South Africans to win power, the question is not how long, but how, if not through armed struggle?

Thenjie arrived as I was about to board the plane. She shoved a white plastic bag into my hand, too hurried to observe the traditional gesture of graciousness: one hand gives, the other touches the extended arm.

On the plane I opened the bag. A long necklace of shiny brown seeds sewn into petaled flower patterns; also, Thenjie's favorite silver earrings.

I was glad I had made the trip. Someday, ANC might give Thenjie a mission inside South Africa. She would change her name, and I might never see her again.

Postscript

Developments in the lives of the people in this book are indicators that conflict in South Africa is moving inexorably toward revolution.

Thenjie In the predawn hours of December 9, 1982, one hundred white South African commandos crossed the Lesotho border and attacked twelve houses in and around Maseru, killing people in their beds and on the streets. Lesotho police said that, in all, thirty members of the ANC and twelve Lesotho citizens were killed. Four black South African exiles were killed across the street from the United States embassy.

Desperate to determine if Thenjie was involved, I phoned Ina Perlman at the Institute of Race Relations in Johannesburg. She found out from local reporters that the house Thenjie had been living in was among those attacked. Ina said Thenjie was apparently out of town at the time.

More than ten months later, Thenjie phoned me from Lesotho. I had been following press reports about the South African government squeezing Lesotho economically, forcing the tiny nation to agree to deport many of the ANC members who had sought refuge within its borders. Negotiations on the matter were being held with United Nations participation. Pretoria had given the Maseru government the names of sixty-eight people it wanted out of Lesotho.

"Obviously I'm on the list," Thenjie said.

Thenjie, who almost never before had mentioned any physical discomfort unless asked, said she had lately been quite sick and unable to eat. "I've lost so much weight. Friends had to carry me to the phone to call you, I'm so weak."

She said that her son Lumumba, then nine years old, was with his father in Swaziland and that she hoped to see him soon. Her mother was still living in the same house on Letsatsi Street in Soweto.

"I would love to come and see you," I said. "No, no," she replied emphatically. Then, as if fearing she might be thought harsh or rude, she added, "Don't do that, I'm living from day to day." She has been doing just that ever since I met her.

I had many questions but she could answer them only obliquely because the phone was probably monitored by South Africa. However, even her elliptical answers indicated the danger she still faces. In a letter five weeks later she spoke of "problems [in] every corner of our lives, my dear." I since learned she has left Lesotho.

Kitty Duma In late 1980, Kitty left South Africa with her four daughters to follow her husband, Enoch, to the United States. Enoch had escaped from his house in Soweto in April 1980, as the police came in the front door to take him away yet again. After hiding out underground for several weeks, he fled across the border into Lesotho, where the U.S. embassy provided him with a visa because he already had an invitation to be a graduate student at the University of Minnesota School of Journalism. He cannot return to South Africa and has applied for permanent residency in the United States. Kitty and her daughters hold passports, so presumably they could return to South Africa for a visit. The littlest daughter, Ntsumi, will grow up with an American accent and will probably speak fractured Zulu and Xhosa.

Cedric Mayson Cedric and his wife, Penelope, were the white couple who introduced me to Thenjie. Now I can tell you about Cedric, for he too has fled South Africa.

A former Methodist minister, Cedric has been editor of a magazine put out by the Christian Institute, a body sympathetic to Black Consciousness and headed by the Afrikaner minister Beyers Naudé. The institute, Cedric, and Beyers were all banned during the crackdown on the Black Consciousness Movement in October 1977.

On November 27, 1981, Cedric was detained before dawn and held incommunicado and without charge for four months. Fifteen months after he was detained he was brought to trial, charged with treason, and accused of furthering the aims of the ANC. During his trial in February 1983 in Pretoria, Cedric testified that while he was in detention, he was mocked for his Christian beliefs, tortured, made to stand naked and handcuffed for sixty hours, and had clumps of hair pulled out of his head. Most unusually, at the request of the prosecutor, the court allowed Cedric to go free on low bail until a missing state witness could be found—a seeming invitation for Cedric to skip the country. He fled through Lesotho and arrived in London in April 1983.

Arthur Benoni Cronwright The chief of interrogation at John Vorster Square who supervised the torture of Enoch Duma was also in charge of Cedric's torture. It was Cedric who suggested to me that I interview Captain Cronwright about his evangelistic Christianity.

Later, Cronwright, promoted to Major, was in charge of the interrogation of trade union leader Neil Aggett, the first white to die under security police detention, in February 1982.

In October 1982 the security police announced that at the end of the year Cronwright would be transferred to the prison at Krugersdorp, west of Johannesburg. This was billed in the press as a demotion, but Krugersdorp prison was already infamous in black nationalist circles for its physical mistreatment of political prisoners.

The missing state's witness in Cedric's trial was an Afrikaner student named Auret Van Heerden. In December 1982, Van Heerden had instituted a 65,000 rand (dollar) claim for damages in court against ten security policemen, including Cronwright, for assault and torture.

Zwelakhe Sisulu Thenjie's friend Zwelakhe, who was president of the Media Workers' Association of South Africa, was issued a three-year banning order in December 1980. In the early hours of June 20, 1981, he was detained and held incommunicado for eight months. Amnesty International designated him a prisoner of the month in October 1981. He was never charged and was released on February 26, 1982, with his banning order still in force.

In the summer of 1983, Zwelakhe's banning orders were lifted, along with those of about sixty others, including his mother, who had been banned successively for many years. In early August, however, security police arrested his mother, sixty-six-year-old Albertina Sisulu, subsequently charging her with furthering the aims of the ANC. The case arose from a funeral in Soweto in January 1982 at which, the prosecution alleged, ANC flags were displayed and songs praising the ANC and its leaders were sung. Shortly after her arrest, the largest antiapartheid rally in twenty-five years was held in Cape Town by the new United Democratic Front organization. Even though she was in prison, Mrs. Sisulu was elected one of the UDF's three leaders. As this book went to press, her trial was moved into secret session after prosecution lawyers said a witness feared for her life. *In-camera* trials prevent press coverage. Her trial was held in Krugersdorp, where Cronwright had been transferred.

Linda Bernhardt Linda married the British man she had been seeing in 1979. A note from her father in early 1983 said she had given birth to a son named Justin, "cute as two buttons, though we nearly lost him at six weeks premature."

In 1981, after a short visit to the United States, Linda had returned to South Africa and, much to her surprise, was escorted straight from Jan Smuts Airport to John Vorster Square police headquarters. She was detained in jail there without charge for a week or so, interrogated, and released. I don't know the reason, excuse, or suspicion that caused her detention because I have not seen her since.

In a letter dated December 1983 Linda spoke of "a really strange, weird, and wonderful two years since my return from the United States. Detention was one story but emerging from that and then having a baby—two extremes of experience." She said she was involved with promoting a couple of exciting new music groups. Politically, she wrote of the growth of a radical white group aligned with the United Democratic Front in opposing the new constitution proposals. "I don't think there has been this much overt political action outside the mainstream parties since '76, and that was mainly black. Prior to that I should imagine one is looking at the fifties with COD (Congress of Democrats). It is quite stimulating to see so many people involved. Whether it will die down now that the November 2 referendum has passed with such an incredible majority (though who could have doubted) remains to be seen."

Helen Suzman Helen described in a letter to me the government's new constitutional proposals, overwhelmingly approved in an all-white referendum November 2, 1983, as resembling the tea party in *Alice in Wonderland.* Her Progressive Federal Party, twenty-seven strong in Parliament, opposed the new measures because blacks were completely ignored by them. Meanwhile, new extreme right-wing Afrikaner groups opposed the proposals because they considered them the first step in the erosion of apartheid, allowing Indians and coloreds a small say in some aspects of government.

Mary Benson Mary was keeping in touch with things South African in 1983 as she always had from London. She had begun to write her autobiography while also working on several radio pieces.

Sheena Duncan Sheena was still speaking eloquently against apartheid, appearing in a *New York Times* page-one feature story on the Black Sash on February 27, 1983, and commenting negatively on the new constitutional proposals on U.S. television late the same year.

Ina Perlman Ina was regional secretary of the Institute of Race Relations in Johannesburg into late 1983, but she hoped to switch full time to a new Institute of Race Relations project called Operation Hunger. In her 1982 institute report she gave one example, like several others, which indicated little had changed under apartheid. "The regional office has also been involved with the car-dump squatters on the Baragwanath Road. This is a tragic community of 134 families who live in disused car and truck hulks on the fringe of Soweto. Most of these people are legally entitled to live in Soweto but have been unable to obtain housing." The institute helped them put their papers in order and found them housing, since the squatters had the means to pay rent. Operation Hunger is, Ina wrote, committed to feeding over half a million people throughout South Africa until March of next year. Drought had drastically affected the country. "We need 150,000 rands (dollars) a month in cash or kind to see us through," she said.

Gabrielle Malan When I phoned Mrs. Malan in mid-October 1983, she said her life had not changed much in the past four years. I told her the title of this book was to be *Cry Amandla!* She was silent a moment and then asked, "Doesn't that mean freedom in Zulu?" It means power, I said. She paused, clearly not pleased. "Well, you did say the book was about women all across the political spectrum." That she could be resigned to such a title was at least an indication that she was not among the most right-wing in the country. She said she was very hopeful for South Africa, especially with the new constitutional proposals, which she enthusiastically supported. "I think the new constitution will ease race relations," she said. But she lamented the very many right-wing Afrikaner groups which she said had sprung up since I had left the country.

Freda Van Rooyen Freda's ebullient voice, with its round, warm tones, sounded the same in mid-October 1983 as when I last talked with her. But—and she forgot to tell me this until the end of our conversation—she had lost half her previous weight. As a result she had more confidence than before. She was no longer much involved with the Kontak organization she had founded, but she had been appointed by the Minister of Internal Affairs to be "chairlady of the Johannesburg Relations Committee." The purpose was "to get colored and other groups to move closer together. It's unbelievable that people say we still don't know each other. South Africa is a fantastic place. People are really trying their utmost. The ordinary people are trying." Freda said she was also a member of the Rand College Board, a colored teachers' training institute. She said the board was working for a breakthrough to get Afrikaners and colored schoolchildren to meet on a social basis. Echoing Mrs. Malan, Freda decried the new right-wing organizations which sprang up to oppose the new constitution.

The lives and attitudes of most of the whites in this book remain virtually unchanged three years after the women first spoke to me. The two blocs of power, Afrikaner and African, are drifting farther apart, if that is possible. Mrs. Malan is still disturbed by the idea of black power and continues to think race tensions can be eased by some tinkering with apartheid. Apartheid is still God's plan. Freda sounds as optimistic as ever that whites and coloreds will solve the country's race problems with social meetings. In grim contrast, the lives of Kitty and Thenjie have been pulled apart at the joints, as is the case with so many blacks and the few white activists who support them.

Apartheid continues to be dolled up with euphemistic phraseology and patched with minuscule concessions. There is no doubt it is alive, well, and barely mutating. The West is doing next to nothing to mitigate the effects of the policy. When we are not actively supporting the status quo, we are passively doing so. That means we are causing mental and physical misery to Thenjie, Kitty, Roslyn, Eunice, Tiny, Hannah, Thamie, Sheena, Ina, Helen, Linda, and Mary, and to millions of people whose stories we will never hear.

APPENDIX A

APPENDIX A

TO: ETHEL TENJIWE MTINTSO
    (I.N. 4421216)
    739 LEIGHTONVILLE
    KING WILLIAM'S TOWN

NOTICE IN TERMS OF SECTION 10QUAT(1) OF THE INTERNAL
SECURITY ACT, 1950 (ACT 44 OF 1950)

WHEREAS there is in force against you a prohibition under

section 9(1) of the Internal Security Act, 1950, by way

of a notice addressed and delivered or tendered to you,

I, JAMES THOMAS KRUGER, Minister of Justice, hereby,

in terms of section 10quat(1) of the said Act order you

for a period commencing on the date on which this notice

is delivered or tendered to you and expiring

on   31 December 1981,   to report to the officer

in charge of the Orlando Police Station, Johannesburg,

on the first Monday   of every month, between

06h00 and 18h00.

Given under my hand at *CAPE TOWN* .this *23 rd*
day of *DECEMBER,*   1976.

[signature]

MINISTER OF JUSTICE

NOTE: The Magistrate,   Johannesburg,   has
in terms of section 10quat(1) of the abovementioned Act
been empowered to authorize exceptions to this notice.

81/172892 (Z 28)

TO: ETHEL TENJIWE MTINTSO
     (I.N. 4421216)
     739 LEIGHTONVILLE
     KING WILLIAM'S TOWN

NOTICE IN TERMS OF SECTION 10(1)(a) OF THE INTERNAL SECURITY
ACT, 1950 (ACT 44 OF 1950)

WHEREAS I, JAMES THOMAS KRUGER, Minister of Justice, am
satisfied that you engage in activities which endanger or are
calculated to endanger the maintenance of public order,
I hereby, in terms of section 10(1)(a) of the Internal Security
Act, 1950, prohibit you for a period commencing on the date
on which this notice is delivered or tendered to you and
expiring on 31 December 1981,   from –

(1) absenting yourself from the **magisterial district of**
     Johannesburg;

(2) being within –
     (a) any Bantu area, that is to say –
          (i)   any Scheduled Bantu Area as defined in
                the Bantu Land Act, 1913 (Act 27 of 1913);
          (ii) any land of which the South African Bantu Trust
                referred to in section 4 of the Bantu Trust and
                Land Act, 1936 (Act 18 of 1936), is the
                registered owner or any land held in trust for
                a Bantu Tribal Community in terms of the said
                Bantu Trust and Land Act, 1936;

- 2 -

   (iii)   any location, Bantu hostel or Bantu village
            defined and set apart under the Bantu
            (Urban Areas) Consolidation Act, 1945
            (Act 25 of 1945);

    (iv)   any area approved for the residence of
            Bantu in terms of section 9(2)(h) of the
            Bantu (Urban Areas) Consolidation Act,
            1945 (Act 25 of 1945);

     (v)   any Bantu Township established under the
            Regulations for the Administration and
            Control of Townships in Bantu Areas, promul-
            gated in Proclamation R293 of 16 November
            1962,

      except Orlando;

(b)   any Bantu compound;

(c)   any area set apart under any law for the occupation
     of Coloured or Asiatic persons ;

(d)   the premises of any factory as defined in the
     Factories, Machinery and Building Work Act,
     1941 (Act 22 of 1941);

(e)   any place which constitutes the premises on
     which any publication as defined in the Internal
     Security Act, 1950, is prepared, compiled,
     printed or published;

- 3 -

(f) any place which constitutes the premises of -

   (i) any organization. contemplated in Government Notice
        R2130 of 28 December 1962, as amended by Government
        Notice R1947 of 27 November 1964;
   (ii)   the South African Students' Organisation (SASO);
   (iii) the Black People's Convention (BPC);
   (iv)   the Black Community Programmes;
   (v)   the South African Students' Movement (SASM);
   (vi)   the Black Parents' Association;
   (vii) the Zimele Trust Fund;
   (viii) the Union of Black Journalists;
   (ix)   the Zizamele Trust Fund;
   (x)   the Soweto Students' Representative Council;

and any place which constitutes premises on which the
premises of any such organization are situate;

(g) any place or area which constitutes the premises on which
     any public or private university, university college,
     college, school or other educational institution
     is situate;

(h) any place or area which constitutes the premises of any
     superior or inferior court as defined in the Criminal
     Procedure Act, 1955 (Act 56 of 1955), except for the
     purpose of -

   (i) applying to a magistrate for an exception to any
        prohibition in force against you under
        the Internal Security Act, 1950;

   (ii) attending any criminal proceedings in which you ar
         required to appear as an accused or a witness;

   (iii) attending any civil proceedings in which you are a
          plaintiff, petitioner, applicant, defendant,
          respondent or other party or in which you are
          required to appear as a witness;

- 4 -

(3) performing any of the following acts -

(a) preparing, compiling, printing, publishing, disseminating or transmitting in any manner whatsoever any publication as defined in the Internal Security Act, 1950;

(b) participating or assisting in any manner whatsoever in the preparation, compilation, printing, publication, dissemination or transmission of any publication as so defined;

(c) contributing, preparing, compiling or transmitting in any manner whatsoever any matter for publication in any publication as so defined;

(d) assisting in any manner whatsoever in the preparation, compilation or transmission of any matter for publication in any publication as so defined;

(e) (i) preparing, compiling, printing, publishing, disseminating or transmitting in any manner whatsoever any document (which shall include any book, pamphlet, record, list, placard, poster, drawing, photograph or picture which is not a publication within the meaning of paragraph (3)(a) above); or

(ii) participating or assisting in any manner whatsoever in the preparation, compilation, printing, publication, dissemination or transmission of any such document,

in which, inter alia -

- 5 -

(aa) any form of State or any principle or
policy of the Government of a State is
propagated, defended, attacked, criticised,
discussed or referred to;

(bb) any matter is contained concerning any
body, organization, group or association
of persons, institution, society or movement
which has been declared an unlawful organization
by or under the Internal Security Act,
1950, or the Unlawful Organizations Act,
1960 (Act 34 of 1960), or any organization
contemplated in Government Notice R2130
of 28 December 1962, as amended by Government
Notice R1947 of 27 November 1964; or

(cc) any matter is contained which is likely
to engender feelings of hostility between
the White and the non-White inhabitants
of the Republic of South Africa;

(f) giving any educational instruction in any manner
or form to any person other than a person of
whom you are a parent;

(g) taking part in any manner whatsoever in the
activities or affairs of -

(i) any organization contemplated in Government
Notice R2130 of 28 December 1962, as
amended by Government Notice R1947 of
27 November 1964;

(ii) the South African Students' Organisation (SASO);
(iii) the Black People's Convention (BPC);
(iv) the Black Community Programmes;
(v) the South African Students' Movement (SASM);
(vi) the Black Parents' Association;
(vii) the Zimele Trust Fund;
(viii) the Union of Black Journalists;

- 6 -

(4) communicating in any manner whatsoever with any
person whose name appears on any list in the custody
of the officer referred to in section 8 of the
Internal Security Act, 1950, or in respect of whom
any prohibition under the Internal Security Act,
1950, or the Riotous Assemblies Act, 1956 (Act 17
of 1956), is in force.

Given under my hand at *CAPE TOWN* this *23 rd*
day of *DECEMBER,* 19*76*.

(signature)

MINISTER OF JUSTICE

NOTE: The Magistrate, **Johannesburg,**   has in
terms of section 10(1)(a) of Act 44 of 1950 been empowered
to authorize exceptions to the prohibitions contained
in this notice.

S1/172892 (Z 28)

TO: ETHEL TENJIWE MTINTSO
      (I.N. 4421216)
      739 LEIGHTONVILLE
      KING WILLIAM'S TOWN

NOTICE IN TERMS OF SECTION 9(1) OF THE INTERNAL SECURITY
ACT, 1950 (ACT 44 OF 1950)

WHEREAS I, JAMES THOMAS KRUGER, Minister of Justice,
am satisfied that you engage in activities which endanger
or are calculated to endanger the maintenance of public
order, I hereby, in terms of section 9(1) of the Internal
Security Act, 1950, prohibit you for a period commencing
on the date on which this notice is delivered or tendered
to you and expiring on   31 December 1981,
from attending within the Republic of South Africa or
the territory of South-West Africa —

(1)   any gathering contemplated in paragraph (a) of the
      said section 9(1); or

(2)   any gathering contemplated in paragraph (b) of the
      said section 9(1), of the nature, class or kind
      set out below:

      (a)   Any social gathering, that is to say, any gathering
            at which the persons present also have social
            intercourse with one another;

- 2 -

(b) any political gathering, that is to say, any gathering
    at which any form of State or any principle or policy
    of the Government of a State is propagated, defended,
    attacked, criticised or discussed;

(c) any gathering of pupils or students assembled for
    the purpose of being instructed, trained or addressed
    by you.

Given under my hand at *CAPE TOWN* this *23 rd*
day of *DECEMBER,* 19*76*.

[signature]

MINISTER OF JUSTICE

Note: The Magistrate, Johannesburg, has
in terms of section 9(1) of the abovementioned Act been
empowered to authorize exceptions to the prohibitions
contained in this notice.

APPENDIX B

WOMEN OUR SILENT SOLDIERS

THE FEDERAL COUNCIL OF THE
NATIONAL PARTY OF
SOUTH AFRICA

Forward Together
NATIONAL

INFORMATION SERVICE

August   1978/79

☆ *Compiled by wives of members of the Cabinet.*

☆ *Edited by G. P. D. Terblanche, M.P.,*
Chief Information Officer of the Federal Council
of the National Party
of 49 Marks Building, Parliament Street, Cape Town.

☆ *Printed by N.G. Sendingpers*
of 39 Blignaut Street, Bloemfontein.

CONTENTS

MRS TINI VORSTER'S CLARION CALL

WOMEN in the National Party are fully aware of the fact that they should not only be interested in the problems as set out in this information document but that they are needed in word and deed in this complex world of today.

Because we as women are believers, we work for our Party. We are conscious of our calling and therefore do our best; and if we do our part for our Party — also through Women's Action — it proves that we are not afraid.

We take cognisance of the most far-reaching decisions ever taken in the history of our Party. We move forward with our menfolk, we demonstrate our loyalty to our Party, we are aware of the circumstances in which we find ourselves — the total onslaught against us as a nation.

With knowledge we can act correctly, show the necessary pluck, we have excellent perception, we are fully aware of political realities and we have correct knowledge of the conditions in our country which will determine our future.

Peace of mind is a priority with us, we as women understand the major role which stability plays in these days. This document will inspire us to continue along with our menfolk in taking the responsibility, to look forward to the future, to ward off everything planned against us.

✧ observe intelligently and ensure that we are informed, because knowledge makes one prepared. For this reason National women must be informed women.

✧ be carriers of a positive attitude and the will to survive to our children and into our community

✧ stay imperturbable and get our priorities in the correct order, because our responsibilities are increasing in scope and intensity and we dare not flinch.

Prime Minister says

OUR PRIME MINISTER SAID:-

"If ever there was a woman in the world's history who was called upon to serve, inspire and support her husband and her child, her nation and her country, then her name is: Woman of South Africa."

— Congress of the S.A. Vrouefederasie, Pretoria, October 1974.

In this document specifically directed to women, the Information Service of the National Party gives a short résumé of important information to put the woman's task in perspective and to help you to help South Africa. A nation's resistance can only be as strong as the resistance which its women can offer.

WOMEN
OUR COUNTRY'S
INVISIBLE WEAPON

WE live in a crucial period characterised by far-reaching changes. The onslaughts against our Fatherland are increasingly becoming more virulent and calculated and the road ahead is becoming more difficult — for these reasons increased service, increased involvement and increased patriotism are required from everybody, particularly also from South African women.

We are engaged in a war, although war has never been declared officially — a war in various spheres, viz. military, economic, psychological-propagandistic and political; and in each sphere we must fight back, which means we must defend ourselves against a total strategy.

It is not only the soldier on the border who has to fight, but each one of us — women are the indispensable "soldiers" within our country's borders and their spiritual power is South Africa's invisible weapon.

Knowledge ensures preparedness

AS WOMEN WE MUST:
   ✪   understand the nature and extent of the onslaught
   ✪   make ourselves available

✿ observe intelligently and ensure that we are informed, because knowledge makes one prepared. For this reason National women must be informed women.

✿ be carriers of a positive attitude and the will to survive to our children and into our community

✿ stay imperturbable and get our priorities in the correct order, because our responsibilities are increasing in scope and intensity and we dare not flinch.

Prime Minister says

OUR PRIME MINISTER SAID:-

"If ever there was a woman in the world's history who was called upon to serve, inspire and support her husband and her child, her nation and her country, then her name is: Woman of South Africa."

— Congress of the S.A. Vrouefederasie, Pretoria, October 1974.

In this document specifically directed to women, the Information Service of the National Party gives a short résumé of important information to put the woman's task in perspective and to help you to help South Africa. A nation's resistance can only be as strong as the resistance which its women can offer.

WOMEN
OUR COUNTRY'S
INVISIBLE WEAPON

WE live in a crucial period characterised by far-reaching changes. The onslaughts against our Fatherland are increasingly becoming more virulent and calculated and the road ahead is becoming more difficult — for these reasons increased service, increased involvement and increased patriotism are required from everybody, particularly also from South African women.

We are engaged in a war, although war has never been declared officially — a war in various spheres, viz. military, economic, psychological-propagandistic and political; and in each sphere we must fight back, which means we must defend ourselves against a total strategy.

It is not only the soldier on the border who has to fight, but each one of us — women are the indispensable "soldiers" within our country's borders and their spiritual power is South Africa's invisible weapon.

Knowledge ensures preparedness

AS WOMEN WE MUST:
  ☆ understand the nature and extent of the onslaught
  ☆ make ourselves available

FIGHT FOR THE SPIRIT OF MAN

THE PSYCHOLOGICAL-PROPAGANDISTIC ONSLAUGHT

THE onslaught against the Republic does not come from the barrel of a rifle or the burst of a bomb only. MUCH, MUCH WORSE!

As far back as 1918 Lenin sent a group of psychologists to the West to study their and also South Africa's way of life, morale of the people, religion, family life and the things that are valued in life. Afterwards he said: **"Now we will destroy the West with the West".**

The psychological-propagandistic campaign against us started at that time and today we still experience it as a fight for the possession of the spirit of man.

> **The Marxists place a much higher value on the spirit of man than the West, because they know that as soon as the people think as they think, the people will believe what they believe, and if a person believes in a cause, rifle fire almost becomes of secondary importance. Because at that stage he is already defeated.**

Communism in S.A.

The Communist Party was banned in South Africa in 1950 but underground they are still co-operating with all the country's enemies in breaking down the image of South Africa and presenting the country as a cruel police state which must be boycotted, to which no weapons may be sold; a country which must be excluded from all world organisations and consequently become totally isolated, so that it will become impossible for us to remain a democratic Christian nation.

The onslaught on morale

A nation's outward power depends on its inner strength and for that reason attempts are being made at all times, in all conceivable ways, in any imaginable sphere of life to attack the nation's morale and make it ludicrous and demolish it. And although these attacks are continually raining on us, they are so subtle that the uninformed person can unconcernedly say that we are suffering from exaggerated fear and are looking for a Communist behind every tree.

Know your enemy

For that reason knowledge is so important. Know your enemy! Knowledge is one of the strongest weapons against Marxism. You cannot fight against your foe unless you know him. Make a study of Marxism in your own family, social or political circles and you will be shocked to learn under what guise the enemy works in the circles in which you move.

Keep your children informed. Live close to them. Warn them in good time. Teach them to be on the look-out for this subtle, psychological propaganda.

Conditioning

The object of the propagandistic assault on our country is to condition our people in such a way that they will lose the will to fight back: to destroy all form of authority, to throw overboard existing values. In short, to demoralise the nation.

Sabotaging the youth

In her book WHAT IS COMMUNISM Gabrielle Malan says in regard to the youth: " . . . The operational

area . . . is particularly the 'weak' . . . the students and the small number of influential and 'free' intellectuals . . . to create a feeling of frustration; aversion to real and artificially created injustices and racial inequality . . . These two groups who have not yet taken sides must be convinced patiently to take sides against the government and government policy. The students are still open to conviction, the intellectuals believe that because of their enlightened view of life, they are in fact impartial and cannot make a choice for or against Communism.''

The psychological and propagandistic onslaught against us is aimed at stirring up fear among our people; at creating dissatisfaction; at rousing mistrust among White, Brown and Black, and in this way preparing the nation for revolution.

This onslaught must be stemmed before the insurrection stage is reached.

Knowledge the countercheck

You can only check this subtle propaganda through knowledge and the truth. Become well-informed and disseminate the correct information at a'l times. It's your task.

ABOVE ALL.

The Marxists deny the existence of God. For that reason breach of faith, immorality, theft, terrorism, sabotage, even murder, is of no importance to them. As long as it furthers their cause.

We recognise God. For that reason we have the complete answer to these onslaughts. However, there is a proviso.

YOU MUST APPLY YOUR KNOWLEDGE. YOU MUST PURPOSELY AND UNSWERVINGLY DO YOUR SHARE IN CHECKING THESE ONSLAUGHTS, OTHERWISE YOU WILL BE A LOSER.

INTERNAL TERRORISM

WHERE DOES IT COME FROM?

AS in the case of all wars the present "war" in South Africa is also the result of political conditions and factors. The military action follows on the political, later to return to the political again.

What does terrorism mean?

The word terrorist means supporter of a reign of terror, or a member of a secret movement fighting the enemy through intimidation, acts of sabotage, violence and even murder.

Terrorism means the demoralisation of a nation through acts of violence with a political objective and it means practising a reign of terror.

Objectives of terrorism

In itself terrorism is not an objective and it can never be successful because it carries the germ of destruction in itself. But the objective of terrorism, whatever form these may take, are to cause chaos and confusion and to subject people to fear; to create a feeling of insecurity. It is an attempt to break down the people's will to resist.

Urban terrorism

Urban terrorism has come to stay for an indefinite period and we will have to learn to live along with this evil, wide awake and on the alert. Urban terrorism inter alia aims at creating a favourable climate for revolution and to bleed our country to death economically. Consider what the Government's costs are to combat infiltration, to maintain certain forces in the operational area, to guard important installations and to fight terrorism in general.

National security

National security is essential for each of us. National security is an indispensable necessity for an independent, self-respecting country which is concerned about the interests of each of its citizens. However, the Republic can only be as safe as its inhabitants wish to make it. Infiltration and subversive action can have no hope of success, provided the community does its duty and helps to combat them. The police and the security forces need the co-operation and support of Whites and Non-Whites.

HUNDREDS OF INSTANCES OF SABOTAGE

Although there have already been several instances of terrorism and hundreds of sabotage, the plans for subversion of the terrorists and saboteurs have time and again been frustrated through timely action by the authorities.

The role of women

The following are examples of counter-offensive action that can be taken.

Whenever a woman engages an employee, she should inter alia pay attention to the following:

a) **Is the identity reference not a falsification? For example, if the number appearing on the document is say 48 million it is obviously a falsification because our Black population is nowhere near that mark.**

b) **Is the photo not a falsification? On a false photo there will will be no perforation, and a person trying to push holes through the photo may damage its fibres.**

c) **Only photos of a person without spectacles are accepted when identity documents are issued.**

Visit their dwelling-places

d) Visit your servant's dwelling places regularly and establish whether strangers are not being harboured there. Be on the look-out for literature of Communist origin. Be particularly on the look-out for books containing a manual for terrorism, and for explosives or formulas for the preparation of explosives.

e) Pay attention to the contents of suitcases and trunks. Inspect for false bottoms in which machine-guns may be smuggled.

f) Pay attention to the clothes worn by your employees. Items which under no circumstances can be obtained in the Republic, e.g. types of shoes, uniforms, overalls, foreign currency, etc. should be reported immediately.

g) Be careful when you receive parcels or when parcels are found in unauthorised places. These may be mail bombs.

h) On the platteland attention must be paid to the surfaces of footpaths that might have been disturbed and be on your guard for objects which you have not seen before.

Banned literature

Banned literature is being distributed regularly and inter alia Black women receive the magazine VOW which is a publication of the banned African National Congress Women's League. Other banned publications for which women can be on the look-out are inter alia the following: The African Communist, Amandla Matla, Vukani Awake, Inkululeko, Sechaba Isiswe and Spotlight on South Africa.

IT IS THE PRIVILEGE OF EVERY WOMAN IN THE COUNTRY TO MAKE HER CONTRIBUTION FOR THE PROTECTION OF HER OWN PEOPLE IN HER OWN UNASSUMING WAY.

WAR ALSO FOUGHT ON THE HOME FRONT

THROUGHOUT our history the South African woman has proved that she was prepared to give her all if her right of existence was threatened. To "rather cross the Drakensberg barefoot" has indeed become a household expression among Afrikaners.

In the *MANCHESTER GUARDIAN* of 15 March 1900 the famous historian, Dr Theal, i.a. wrote the following about the South African Boer woman:

> "Boer women fervently urge their menfolk to continue the war to the bitter end. For the sake of their independence the Boer women will send out and encourage their husbands and son after son to preserve in the struggle until the end. They are comforted by their unswerving belief in God and the righteousness of their cause. The men are what the women have made of them."

The home front

South Africa is at the present time involved in the most severe struggle for existence in its entire history. The onslaught comes from all sides and sources and is reasoned and complicated; friends of the past have become enemies; those who seek our downfall make no secret of this.

> The waging of war has become an intricate game in which the use of sophisticated weapons is but a single aspect. War is not being waged on the battlefield only, but also on the home front and finds expression in the polarisation of people and groups, in the international arena, in the cultural and economic spheres — even on the sports fields.

If we wish to wage this war and win it we will need determination and perseverance as never before. And it is exactly here where the woman and mother of South Africa plays a decisive role:

We must be able to identify the sting in the calculated onslaughts against our moral defences, to call it by name and to render it harmless. For that reason it is essential that we shall continually be well-informed on what is happening in the world around us.

Attempts at isolating South Africa in the international sphere are being made every day, because it is an efficacious method to overwhelm them. Every woman must endeavour to break through this isolation on the individual as well as the national level. Much can be achieved through personal contact.

Civil defence

More than ever before, we now need an unshakeable belief in God and the righteousness of our cause. Every woman must strive at setting an example by treating every fellow South African, irrespective of the racial group from which he or she comes, as a human being without allowing herself to be intimidated into a position where she begins apologising for her very existence.

> In everyday life every woman also has a duty to do. During emergencies as well as during times of prosperity and peace she must be prepared to render service wherever required. In fact, participation in Civil Defence activities is necessary. Also the drawing up of an emergency plan. Do you know your neighbours in order that you will be able to co-operate with them during emergencies?

On the battlefield

On the war front, on the battlefield, women also have a major contribution to make. It is their courage, zeal, perseverance and fervour which will encourage and inspire our men on the border to defend our country and safeguard our frontiers.

Every woman must do her duty in her own household so that her husband without being worried can serve in uniform — or are you the millstone round his neck? Are you capable of fending for yourself when it comes to sales tax, income tax forms, insurance premiums, etc.?

A woman's most important task is the educational task. A child develops pride in his cultural assets, his language, his nation and his country largely through his mother's guidance.

> **Is compulsory military service an obligation of honour and a privilege of every citizen — or would we rather send the neighbour's son to defend us? Is our daughter aware of her role in defence in order that she can inspire her brother or friend in uniform with pride?**

Struggle for existence

We will have to do with less, so that we will have more to give to the defence effort. Every woman will have to make the nation's struggle for existence a personal struggle for existence.

WHAT CAN YOU AND I DO TO HELP?

★ **We can buy defence bonds**

★ **We can support the Southern Cross Fund which helps to augment the Defence Force Fund**

★ **We can support an organisation which aims at making life for our men on the border more comfortable.**

Each of us is also "doing service" — not for 12, 18 or 24 months, but every day. We are "doing service" without call-up instructions, without military pay, but in service of the things which are dear to us — our families, our country, our nation.

SOUND RELATIONS

OPPORTUNITIES FOR EVERYBODY

THE creation of sound relations between nations in South Africa is a matter of top priority. It calls for positive and responsible action from every nation, every leader and every individual. It requires a large amount of goodwill between national groups or individuals from the different national groups.

It demands that the conduct of the individual shall under all circumstances be above reproach. Inconsiderateness, rudeness and insulting language do more harm than can be imagined.

IN ALL SERIOUSNESS THE PRIME MINISTER PUTS IT AS FOLLOWS:

> "Your conduct must not come from a feeling of superiority. Your attitude should be that on the one hand there are not inferior nations, and on the other hand no superior nations. Admittedly there are less-developed nations, nations with different views on morality, on what is permissible. There is a difference in civilisation and insight, but these differences must not induce you to take the viewpoint that you can raise yourself as being superior to other nations."

> **— Before Rapportryers in Port Elizabeth on 30/9/1976.**

Certain hostile parties come with accusations that the White man — and by name the Afrikaner — committed an injustice to the Brown and Black nations because the Afrikaner has looked after his own interests only. These parties then come and shout: "You must share your wealth with others."

No injustice committed

Here too our Prime Minister gives sound advice to every national group, every individual and every leader:

> "You must create chances and opportunities for all people to attain what you have attained and it is your Christian duty, wherever you may be and under all circumstances, to lend a helping hand."
> — Port Elizabeth 30/9/1976.

THE PRIME MINISTER THEN CONTINUES:

> "The accusation against the Afrikaner would have been true if we had neglected the schooling and education of the other national groups or had refused to make it possible for their children to receive tuition and education."
> — Port Elizabeth 30/9/1976.

Opportunities are plentiful — the authorities are doing their duty. All the opportunities for training and education are available to every individual from every national group or nation.

> "To lead a successful life does not depend on what other people do, does not depend on the viewpoints of other people — the gaurantee for success is what you yourself believe, what you yourself is prepared to do and what you in point of fact do."
> —Prime Minister at Pearston High School, 31/6/1976.

Relations improved in this way

★ **Sound relations between nations** are thus being promoted through joint and continued efforts of every national group or nation, of every individual and of every leader to exploit opportunities in order that attributes of quality of every individual can be advanced.

★ **Sound relations between nations** are also being promoted when full and equal opportunities are made available to every person. When this is not the case, one feeds the hungry soul with frustration and hate which will culminate in confrontation.

★ **Sound relations between nations** are being promoted when every national group or nation, every individual and every leader show less arrogance and a greater measure of positive action — that means genuine efforts at building bridges and not at demolishing them through negative conduct.

"What we are going to do, however, is to afford every individual in his national context, every member of every community, the opportunities to develop to the full, to preserve his human dignity at all times and to work out for him and his children a full and equal place in the sun in South Africa."

— Prime Minister, Hansard 1977, col. 5609

Facilities for all

WHAT IS THE POSITION AT PRESENT?

1. All population groups have schools with equivalent sullabuses.
2. Today everybody has access to a university.
3. Adequate dining and travelling facilities are provided or aimed at.
4. The Government is giving its urgent attention to the narrowing or elimination of the wage gap. In view of the urgency of the matter the Government has ordered that a system be devised in terms of which categories of officials shall be compiled in order to eliminate the gap according to a fixed pattern.
5. On the sports field it was the National Party's policy of separate development which provided the opportunities for people of different colours to compete against one another.
6. Constitutionally the Government is giving the Brown man and the Asian the opportunity of having discussions with the White man on a new political dispensation, viz, of having the only say in matters relating to themselves and. co-responsibility in matters of common concern.

The Black nations have all been put on the road to independence. The urban Black people are receiving the urgent attention of the Government as regards their development. In addition the Minister of Plural Relations is busy with a five-year plan to make Soweto "the most beautiful Black city in Africa."

Millions for housing

7. **Housing:** The National Government has an excellent record as regards the provision of housing through Community Development and local authorities:

1949-1977	Number of dwelling units completed	Cost
Whites	99 726	R655 505 000
Coloureds	176 886	R497 470 000
Indians	51 707	R167 897 000
Black people	493 274 (1950-1977)	R377 500 000 (1968-1977)

As regards the Coloureds it can be mentioned that the 35 645 dwelling units which are being built at present, will ensure that the shortage will in future decrease at a strongly accelerated rate.

As regards the Indians, the 20 220 dwelling units completed during the past five years as well as the 12 234 dwelling units which are being built at present, will largely help to alleviate the housing needs of Indians considerably.

The squatter problem

Since 1975 when Community Development started with the clean-up of squatter camps in the Western Province, 6 588 squatter families were provided with alternative accommodation after which the shanties were demolished, which brought the number of shanties standing at 31 December 1977 to 17 395.

Strict control to prevent illegal squatting is still being exercised by the various local authorities. The present building as well as the large schemes for Mitchell's Plain should make it possible for the authorities to do away with the remaining 17 395 shanties towards the end of 1983.

As far as Blacks are concerned it can be mentioned that the Administration Boards concerned are giving positive attention to the clean-up of squatter camps where Black people are settled in large numbers. The clean-up is undertaken in close collaboration with the Departments of Plural Relations and Community Development. Where permanent housing is not available immediately, those concerned are temporarily accommodated in a transit camp.

Home ownership

The new plan to give Black people more security through home ownership, that is the new leasehold system, contains many possibilities for the better. Home ownership is facilitated and becomes more assured. It creates a pride in and a will to protect one's own possessions.

The most significant aspect of the new dispensation for Blacks is that Black people will obtain greater security as regards occupation, which will for example make it more practical for building societies to grant bonds to Black people to acquire their own homes or to enlarge them.

Peaceful labour relations

The peaceful labour relations with which South Africa has been blessed for so many years and which stand in glaring contrast to the incessant strikes in European and other Western countries, have always been one of the corner-stones of South Africa's continued development. For that reason it would amount to absolute foolishness to do anything which could jeopardise this peace. As Mr Fanie Botha, Minister of Labour, said: **"A prosperous South Africa will be built on sound labour relations."**

But to build a prosperous South Africa it will be necessary to use the available labour optimally, which will call for certain adjustments such as the doing away with obsolete and useless practices.

There is a shortage of White workers, while Brown, Yellow and Black workers are waiting to be employed. With this in view certain changes have already been made to industrial legislation and more can come after the Wiehahn Commission has completed its work.

Liaison committees

There is a big responsibility, not only on the Government, but on every person who means well with our country, to promote sound and peaceful intergroup and man-to-man relations for the sake of peace and order in our Fatherland. This is a never-ending task, which in addition calls for patience, common sense, skill and dedication.

The Department of Coloured Relations took the initiative in this regard three years ago with the establishment of a structure of Public Liaison Committees. White and Coloured leaders, locally recognised in a variety of spheres, serve in these committees.

At present there are more than 100 such committees which have already done an enormous amount of work in eliminating unnecessary points of friction in relations at local level. A recent country-wide survey disclosed how relations between Whites and Coloureds have improved during the past number of years.

Organisations queried

There are other organisations, such as **"WOMEN FOR PEACE"**, **"WOMEN'S MOVEMENT"** and **"WOMEN FOR PEACEFUL CHANGE NOW"** which profess that they are also furthering relations work among women, but whose **modus operandi** are questioned strongly.

> **Their actions are questioned because they were not long in making demands amounting to educational integration and other forms of integration, which most certainly will not improve relations. The names of some of the persons involved also pointed to a distinct P.F.P. connection.**

"KONTAK", another women's organisation which is active in relations work, has failed to make use of and co-ordinate with the guidance and expertise of the Government's relations structure, in spite of undertakings in this regard.

The Department of Coloured Relations has stationed eight relations officers in different regions, and their assistance and guidance are at all times available to women who wish to undertake relations work.

TALK ENTHUSIASTICALLY ABOUT THE N.P.

IN these stressing and challenging times in which we live it is imperative that women shall act positively and directively in the National Party.

The National Party has just celebrated the thirtieth anniversary of its coming into power. It is inconceivable that this could have been achieved without the active support and contribution of women.

> **The struggle continues and intensifies, and for that reason an even greater measure of loyalty, support and enthusiasm will be required of our women. If your contribution of yesterday proved to be important, your share for tomorrow is of decisive importance.**

The National Party is the only political instrument which can ensure a safe future for South Africa and all its peoples; and for the sake of those to whom we wish a future, it is worth while furthering the cause of the National Party.

Don't tattle

It is of the utmost importance that your National convictions and sentiments shall continually be interwoven with the world in which you live and whatever you may say or do. A woman who can talk and chat enthusiastically about the National Party, makes the interests of her party part of her very existence, and this stimulates those people who are still on the touch-lines. One must live out and experience what one professes.

★ Steer clear of polite tattling with those who are uninformed or unsympathetic. Critical discussions are fruitful but tattling is counterproductive and dangerous.

Play an active part

★ Demonstrate your enthusiastic simpathy and support by playing an active part in the party organisation in your constituency. Because of your contribution on branch committee level you need not hesitate and indeed have the right also to expect it from others. The branch is the nurturing ground for knowledge on political and policy matters and stimulates one to attend conferences and congresses in a wider sphere.

★ Take cognisance of general political developments but be well informed on the National Party and its policy and implementation of the policy.

Nurture your children politically

★ Your children are your most important responsibility. Educate them politically so that they will not later become part of a confused and apathetic group of young people. Get as many as possible of them involved in party activities because this will result in only a very small number of them at university for example being drawn away from the National fold by foreign dogmas and left/liberal schools of thought. A political conciousness must be cultivated from an early age so that as they grow up, it will become part of their way of life, of their character and of their convictions.

Racial relationships

Whatever you practise must and also will affect others, but it requires positive action and an example worthy of imitation.

What is the national woman's contribution in this regard?

She must make full use of the opportunities in helping to promote good racial and national relationships.

None of us need have a guilt complex towards people of a different skin colour, because it is none other than the National Party which has created opportunities for the Coloured, the Indian and the Black man and has fostered a feeling of self-esteem and consciousness of identity among them.

By showing a normal interest in people of a different skin colour and by acting correctly and decently towards them, they will not become estranged and be driven to people engaged in influencing them by foreign ideologies.

Sympathetic interest

Sympathetic interest in our employees, also as regards their domestic circumstances, needs and problems, creates a general humane atmosphere which elicits appreciation. In this way they will also become to trust their employers, which in turn will yield positive results.

Employees and servants must not merely be seen as workers only, but they must be seen in their family context and above all in their national context.

Own fatherlands

We are dealing with Black people with their own Fatherlands. Surely that is the basis of National Party policy. We can help by stimulating them to take pride in that fatherland, their language, traditions and customs and a consciousness of own identity.

Opportunities for making contact with people of their own nation, also in their own Black states, should be encouraged and created deliberately. Information concerning their own country, the leaders there and events and developments leading to progress or advancement of the country and in-information on settlement in the Black states should be brought to their attention at all times.

Knowledge of a Bantu language facilitates communication and helps people to understand each other's problems.

Index

About the Author

June Goodwin has been a journalist for sixteen years, affiliated with *The Christian Science Monitor*, National Public Radio, and Reuters news agency. She collected these interviews while she was in South Africa for the *Monitor*. In 1977 she was given the Overseas Press Club Madeline Dane Ross award for international reporting that shows a concern for humanity. She now lives in Oberlin, Ohio, where she is writing fiction.

Date Due

DIS   MAY 0 7 1998   MAY 0 8 1998

CIRC JUL 1 0 1985

DIS JUL 0 2 1985   DIS CIRC MAY 1 1 1996

CIRC JUN - 9 1986   DIS APR 2 7 1998

DIS JUN 5 1986

ILL   DIS SEP 2 3 1992

DIS JUL 2 7 1986   MAY 9 1995

CIRC DEC 4 1987   DIS   OCT 2 3 1995

Jan 5 MAY 1 5 2002

DIS NOV 2 8 1995

DIS JAN 1 3 1988

CIRC NOV 4 1988 JUN 1 0 1999

DIS OCT 2 7 1988 DIS MAY 1 1 1996

DIS JUL 2 3 1996

CIRC MAY 0 6 1989 MAY 1 4 1992

MAY 2 0 1999

CIRC MAY 3 0 1989

MAY 0 4 2004

DEC 0 4 2001